HEDGEHOG
FIRST AID

A practical guide to hedgehog care and rehabilitation

by

ANGELA SMITH

Hedgehog
First Aid

A practical guide to hedgehog care and rehabilitation

by

Angela Smith

ISBN: 978-0-9559681-0-5

This book is also available spiral bound. Please telephone +44 (0)1582 730896

Published by AM Smith in conjunction with Writersworld Limited,

Printed and bound by printondemand-worldwide.com

www.writersworld.co.uk

WRITERSWORLD
2 Bear Close
WOODSTOCK
Oxfordshire
OX20 1JX
England

Front cover photograph:

A young hog found clinging to a rock in a drainage ditch suffering from pneumonia, dehydration, hypothermia and exhaustion. After a few weeks of care it was successfully released back into the wild.

Foreword

Have you ever found a hedgehog that you think is sick or injured and needs help? How do you know if it really needs assistance? Would you know the best course of action to take? Could you nurse it back to health?

This book is intended to help anyone who finds themselves in this situation and to set them on the path to becoming a hedgehog carer.

It will guide you through all the stages in the care of a sick or injured hedgehog, from initial first aid, medical treatment and rehabilitation, to releasing it back into the wild.

This book will also serve as a handy reference guide with answers to many commonly asked questions on a wide range of hedgehog behaviour.

Acknowledgements

Many thanks to the following, whose invaluable assistance has enabled this book to be written in an accurate and user-friendly way.

Robert Smith   my husband:
for editing, proof reading and support

Catherine Hughes   B.Vet.Med., M.R.C.V.S:
for taking the time to check and clarify
medical procedures

Melanie Seeliger   M.R.C.V.S:
for taking the time to check and clarify
medical procedures

Jackie Burke   Carer:
for working with the first draft copy and drawing
attention to points for clarification

The public   whose financial support has enabled Caddington
Hedgehogs to continue operating

Contents

Reference

Limbs/toes/claws	22, 23, 24, 25, 56, 61, 77, 90
Lumps/swellings	21, 31
Movement/unusual behaviour	41, 57, 58, 59, 71, 82, 89
Nests	40, 43, 50, 51, 58, 60, 68, 69, 73
Parasites	8, 9, 10, 11, 12, 13, 14, 18, 33, 34, 35
Releasing/relocating	48, 50, 61, 62, 63, 87, 88, 92
Sexing	42
Skin problems	36, 44, 45, 77, 78
Snout/mouth	26, 27, 35
Spines	7, 29, 30, 36
Toileting	75, 77, 78, 80
Weaning	85
Wounds	18, 19, 20, 22, 36, 45, 55

Introduction

You may ask yourself 'what is the point of nursing a sick hog back to health; surely it is nature's way of ensuring only the fittest survive?' I could accept this point of view if it were not for the reasons why the hogs are brought in.

Only a handful of hogs come in to my care as runts that stand absolutely no chance of survival, or as Autumn orphans born too late in the season to gain sufficient weight to hibernate. Most come in with injuries caused by dog attacks, garden forks and strimmers, blows to the head causing prolapsed eyes, entrapment in rubbish or outbuildings, poisoning, falling into ponds or uncovered drains, orphaned because the mother has died (quite often flattened on the road), or horrific burns from hibernation sites that became bonfires.

The list goes on and on, all problems caused by humans, many being quite avoidable. It seems only right, therefore, that we try and redress the balance by nursing these very inoffensive creatures, even if only a handful, back to health and returning them to where they belong, in the wild.

Unfortunately, it is a harsh reality that if a problem is not identified and treatment started within the first 24 hours, it is often too late to do anything. It is a sad statistic, but 70 % of hogs born in the wild in a year are thought not to make it to adult independence.

I started Caddington Hedgehogs in 2003 with the intention of caring for distressed hogs found by the general public and from vets. It soon became apparent that simply giving food and a bed was not going to be enough for many of the casualties that came through my hands, and that more expert advice was required, mainly through veterinary intervention.

I was uncertain as to how I would be received and if indeed my services were actually required. Those fears were quickly laid to rest as the hogs started to flood in. At the time of writing this book I have taken in over 1,000 hogs, just under half of which have been returned to the wild.

It has been a steep learning curve and I would dearly love to have a second chance at some of the hogs that came in during my first year. I am sure many more could have been saved with the knowledge and experience gained during the ensuing years.

When I started to write this book I had no idea it would be so complex or take so long to compile. It seemed that for every hedgehog problem covered, another two would spring to mind. How a wild creature that has been on this planet since prehistoric times can suffer from so many problems and still be around just amazes me.

This book has a large question-and-answer, problem-solving section from which you will be able to 'pick-and-mix' information easily and quickly in order to accurately assess a hog's health and know how best to treat it. Thoughts and ideas change through new research. Each carer will have their own way of tackling problems and as new drugs are used successfully on hogs, our armoury increases.

Bear in mind from day one, hedgehog care is not something that can be undertaken without the help of a vet. All problems should be referred to your vet the first time you come across them as, without experience, you will probably not be aware of what is a life-threatening situation and what is one that can successfully be treated by yourself.

I am very fortunate in having access to a wonderful veterinary practice who take my "hobby" seriously and who bend over backwards to try and accommodate the many no-hopers that are continually taken in expecting miracles to be performed on their tiny broken bodies. I am sure that they are as disappointed as myself, when after having worked so hard, perhaps over many weeks, we finally have to admit defeat and the hog has to be put to sleep. This only magnifies the feeling of euphoria when a hog has been pulled back from the brink and is finally released into its natural habitat, hopefully to reproduce and create many more little hoglets.

I have drawn a line at what the vet may be able to do. Every veterinary practice is different and some may have a keener interest in wildlife than others.

You may be charged for veterinary care. You must bear in mind that vets are running a business and they have to pay bills and balance books like any other business, and to continually give treatment for free would be impractical and not economically sound. If you do get free treatment, accept it as a one-off and don't be offended if you are charged for your next visit. Since I started, I have spent thousands of pounds on veterinary care: I am certain I have received far more consultations and medication than this accounts for.

Some very important questions need to be asked if you are going to set yourself up as a hedgehog carer:

- How are you going to finance your work?

- Will you be able to offer 24-hour cover for emergency veterinary treatment (in particular, euthanasia)?

- Will you save all hogs, even those that cannot be released back into the wild? You could become inundated with non-releasable hogs that take up all your time and resources, thus creating a situation where you don't have space for casualties.

- How are you going to dispose of bodies and waste material? When I first set up I took all our animal-waste and bedding to the local tidy-tip. However, regulations for waste now prohibit this type of disposal. I now hire a bin from the local Council to take all the clinical waste created, together with any bodies, for proper disposal by incineration.

- Are you going to collect sick animals from the public yourself?

Please be careful if going out to people you do not know, especially at night; your safety is the first and most important thing to think about.

If you are going to allow people into your garden with sick hogs or if you fundraise, then I advise you to seek *Public Liability* insurance cover. If you have helpers, you will require *Employers' Liability* cover (even if you are not paying them a wage). Finding an insurance company willing to cover you is a major task in itself.

These are just a few pointers to bear in mind. It can be extremely frustrating trying to offer a service to the public and all you come up against is red tape that not only costs you time sorting out, but can cost you a great deal of money.

Having said all that, I hope I have not put you off getting involved with these charming, if contradictory, creatures.

You will be best advised to contact the following organisations to register on their database and to find out if there are any other hog carers in your area who might be able to give you some pointers.

Keep a note of their details at the back of this book on **page 75** so you can easily find them again when required.

British Hedgehog Preservation Society (BHPS)

01584 890801

Website address: www.britishhedgehogs.org.uk

Hedgehog Helpline

01495 244149

02920 623985

Spike's World

01522 688300

Publicity and fund raising

You will need to advertise your phone number. Contacting BHPS, Hedgehog Helpline and Spike's World should be your first steps; see phone numbers on previous page.

You could then try contacting your local vets, schools, newspapers, libraries, church/parish magazines. Try putting a leaflet or booklet together and sending it out to people or organisations you think might be interested.

Once you have a list of contacts, you could offer to give talks on hedgehogs for a donation of either food or cash. Ask at your local schools if you could have a stall at their fete or Christmas Bazaar. Suggest via your parish magazine that donations of food could be offered by your local community on a regular basis, thus releasing funds to pay for vet bills and equipment.

Medication and equipment

Most of the drugs that have been proven effective for hedgehogs are only available from the vet and are usually either prescription-only or controlled drugs, and so appointments are necessary to obtain them.

Listed on this page and highlighted are a few 'pills and potions' that can be purchased either from your local pharmacy or from your vet. They may have to be ordered for you, so ensure you give plenty of notice if you require something on a regular basis.

- **Abidec:** baby vitamins (pharmacy)
- **Aloe Vera gel + vitamin E:** for baby hogs' skin (supermarket)
- **Charcoal tablets:** for diarrhoea (pharmacy or health shop)
- **Esbilac:** milk substitute (Spike's World) or **Cimivit** (vet)
- **Fennel tea** (health food shops)
- **HiBiscrub:** antimicrobial wash for wounds (pharmacy)
- **Hydrogen peroxide 6 %** (pharmacy)
- **Johnson's Rid-Mite:** pyrethrum-based spray for birds, kills mites and fleas (pet shops or Spike's World)
- **Milton:** sterilising solution or tablets (supermarket or pharmacy)
- **Olbas oil:** to aid breathing (pharmacy or health shop)
- **Optrex:** eye bath for flushing out debris from eyes (pharmacy)
- **Panacur 10 %:** liquid wormer (vet)
- **SA37:** vitamins (pet shop)
- **Tea-tree** ointment: for cracked skin (pharmacy or health shop)
- **Tubigauze** (pharmacy or supermarket)

A detailed list of prescription drugs and their dosage can be obtained from BHPS. This important list should accompany you each time you visit the vet so that they have ready access to what can be used and the correct dosage required.

The following items are what I have found to be invaluable in the care and treatment of hedgehogs:

- Baby-feeding bottles (Spike's World)
- Booking-in forms and clip board
- Buckets
- Chicken cat food in jelly (must be good quality)
- Cotton buds
- Cotton wool (for drizzling HiBiscrub into wounds)
- Digital scales
- Heat mats (AC-mains powered, from Spike's World)
- Iams Senior chicken cat food
- Lantern/torch (rechargeable, for checking animals at night)
- Latex gloves
- Liquidiser (for producing pureed food)
- Measuring jug
- Newspaper (for bottom of cages)
- Paper kitchen towel
- Pet bowls (not saucers as they tend to be flipped over by the hog)
- Plastic pipettes (good for flushing out debris from eyes and feeding fluids to sick hogs; from craft shops)
- Rabbit hutch

- Rabbit run
- Reading glasses (off-the-counter low strength, to magnify what you are working on)
- Scissors, sharp & small (for snipping spines/dead skin/netting)
- Spike's World dried food
- Straw (for bedding)
- Street maps of your local area (for directions to pick-up locations)
- Tea towels or dish cloths (for cleaning)
- Tick-removing gadget (O'TOM tick remover from the vet is most effective)
- Towels (for handling and bedding)
- Tweezers (good quality, fine-pointed for removal of maggots and debris from wounds)
- Weetabix
- Wood-chip (for floor of rabbit run)

Basic care for hogs in captivity

Hedgehogs are classified as insectivores. That being said, they are brilliant opportunists and will eat almost anything that is left lying around. It has been reported that they will eat fledgling birds that have fallen out of nests and carcases of dead animals. Fruit put out for my tortoise has been consumed by my blind hog. They are also well-known for eating the crumbs from under bird tables. Many an underweight hog has survived the winter simply by visiting these food stations.

They are very keen on beetles and grubs but don't appear to like the large slugs that come out at night. Although they will eat snails and small slugs they prefer something fast moving like ground-beetles and millipedes; woodlice do not appear to be very palatable to them. Obviously milk and bread are definitely off the menu as they can cause diarrhoea.

So what should you feed your sick hog?

A first thought would logically be to give it what you can find in the garden. Three problems arise from this theory. One, it is extremely time-consuming—a hog can eat one-third of its body weight in an evening. Two, some hedgehog parasites spend part of their life-cycle living in things like slugs, snails, worms and beetles. Giving an already weakened hog contaminated food could vastly increase the background burden of parasites it is probably already carrying. Three, any mini-beast you find lying around could easily be dying of some kind of pesticide and so would not be a good idea as a meal.

Good quality food is a must; tinned chicken cat food in jelly is very attractive to hogs. Into this, mix one *Weetabix* (or cheap equivalent) together with one pinch of *SA37* per hog. The *Weetabix* provides the necessary roughage a hog would get from the exoskeleton of insects.

This is fed at night time, when there are no flies around to lay eggs on the meat.

During the day, give *Spike's World dried food*. Even hogs with few teeth seem to relish this as a meal. If the hog is desperately underweight it might be best to give it a high protein food. This is also a good idea if the animal is only eating small amounts; keep *Iams Senior chicken cat food* in stock for just this type of emergency. The animal should quickly gain weight. When it has reached a healthy state, remove this food and revert back to the tinned cat food or *Spike's World dried food*, otherwise you will be in danger of creating an obese animal.

A good point to bear in mind if the hog is underweight and ill, is always ensure there is food in its bowl, day and night. If it has reached a healthy weight and you are simply waiting for spines to re-grow or wounds to heal, food during the day should be kept down to only 5 or 6 pieces of dried food, just in case it wakes up hungry. After all, the hog should not be encouraged to feed during the day, but to come out at night.

With healthy hogs, make them wait for their evening meal. A hog can naturally wander between 2 and 3 miles a night in its home range. If you are keeping it in a rabbit run or hutch then it is very quickly going to get bored. If you allow it to root around for a while in wood-chip placed on the floor of the run, it will be getting valuable exercise and mental stimulation. Giving extra bedding also encourages natural behaviour.

Provide fresh water at all times.

Clean the food bowls out daily with *Milton* sterilising solution. Wipe the food bowl and dry with kitchen roll. This reduces the possibility of passing on infections from one hog to another through contaminated food bowls. When the hog no longer needs its bowl, wash and soak the bowl in Milton overnight before re-use.

What is a sick hog?

In order to identify a sick animal and try to understand what its problems are, it is best to know what is classed as normal behaviour.

Hogs should only be out and active during late evening under cover of darkness and very early morning, returning to the protection of their nest site as dawn breaks. They rarely stay still for more than a few moments and may even appear hyperactive in their never-ending quest for food. They have a wet nose, bright black eyes, clean fur under their bodies and a good covering of spines on top of their body; they tend to smell like compost heaps, nice and earthy. They walk in a flat-footed fashion and have five digits to each foot. The males urinate in short bursts over a few seconds.

Hogs can usually be persuaded to uncurl for very short periods (namely seconds), but they will obviously object most strongly to any intrusive examination. The ones that flatly refuse to even entertain the idea of uncurling are usually in a desperate state. Going one step further, if it appears to be hibernating during the summer months, i.e. it is cold, tightly curled up and only moving slightly to your touch, the problem is quite often too severe to rectify. A hog in true hibernating state, if disturbed, will appear to swell in size, bristle its spines and possibly emit a loud breathing sound, rather like bellows being drawn.

A normal hog's droppings should look black, thin and long with a tapered end, rather like cat faeces. Their nests are similar to mice nests and they often site them under frame-like structures, such as sheds, decking, tarpaulin or brambles. Any hog out and curled up in an exposed area is experiencing difficulties.

More than one hog may visit the same garden in an evening but at different times. It has been noted that several nest sites may be made in their home range. Unoccupied nests might be used by other hogs, hence the ability for ticks and fleas to spread from one hog to another. Hogs have a tendency to defecate in or just outside their own nest, probably informing other hogs of that site's occupancy.

It is well-known that a hog will curl up if disturbed. If a hog senses danger it will first freeze for a few seconds, listening to what is going on around it, ready to make a split-second decision regarding what course of action to take. It might choose to amble off if it feels no threat, frown in protection of its face if unsure, or curl up into a ball as a last means of defence. They do not tend to bite.

Wild hogs may use their teeth to drag each other by the spines when tempers are high. One orphaned baby I was hand-rearing succeeded in giving such a severe bite to its sibling's foot that it was in danger of losing some toes, though I suspect that the reason was more to do with curiosity than outright aggression.

Hogs do not usually fight unless they get too close to each other. Like humans, they don't like their body space being invaded. Fighting can take the form of quacking rather like a duck, huffing, biting of spines, dragging of opponent and shunting with their head. These are also the characteristics of a mating couple, with the added behaviour of circling by the male to head off any chance of escape by the female.

Hogs only appear to protect their immediate vicinity, working along the lines of what they don't see doesn't hurt. It is not thought that hogs scent-mark. However I have seen on many occasions a hog rub its chin along the ground rather like a cat rubbing its jowls against a raised object in an obvious act of territorial marking. Whether this is to allow the hog to find its way back, tell others of its existence, or a sexual gesture to announce availability of the female or masculinity of the male, is a question I have been unable to answer.

A trait unique to hogs is *self-anointing* and is perfectly normal (see **page 70**). It is not known why this is done but the trigger appears to be new or strong tastes. When hand-rearing babies, the introduction of meat into their diet or the first experiences of the leather strap on your watch are almost guaranteed to set into motion this very unusual behaviour. They will show a frantic interest in what they have found, chewing and licking the object frenziedly, followed by a smacking of the mouth and flicking of saliva over their spines, contorting into some very disturbing body shapes to enable cover of as large an area as possible.

To distract them from this behaviour is futile and unnecessary; they soon calm down after a few minutes and resume their normal daily activities.
I have only observed self-anointing by hogs growing into adults while in captivity, but not by adults newly admitted into care.

Nest building appears to be instinctive. Babies of only a few weeks of age have been given bits of tissue which they have eagerly taken into their mouths and after some confusion as to what to do with it, deposited it into their nests.

Hogs are very good at escaping. They can climb fences and chicken wire, scale uneven walls, dig under and squeeze between, obstacles. To understand, and therefore prevent a hog in care from escaping, think of it as a rather large hamster. If you think a hamster could escape from the enclosure it is almost certain a hog will. They are not the bumbling, uncoordinated clumsy creatures they appear to be. Their long legs are concealed beneath their furry skirts. I have lost count of the people who have telephoned with an animal in obvious difficulties, first aid advice given, only for the caller to ring back to say it had vanished during the phone call. Their reaction is usually the same, that of disbelief, almost as if they thought it had performed some kind of magician's disappearing trick. A hog can successfully be contained in a plastic storage box of about 35 cm in height.

14

Problems can be age-related, so trying to ascertain how old it is can help point to what is wrong. The first 18 months are fairly easy to judge. They start to gain their white spines about 1 hour after being born. The white spines are outnumbered by darker spines at about 5 days old.

They start to practise curling into a ball at 11 days, eyes and ears start to open at 2 weeks. At 3 weeks their teeth start to emerge. At 4 weeks a good covering of fur on their tummies has formed and they are also less jerky in their walking.

At 6 weeks their snouts have started to protrude, at 8 weeks they may be on their own, weighing about 350 gm. I keep them in captivity till 450 gm to give them as good a chance as possible in the wild. They have two sets of teeth, the first set being the baby teeth which they start to gain at about 3 weeks and lose at about 4 months. The second set stay with them for life. The only accurate method to tell the age of a hog is to take a cross-section of their jaw bone and count the rings, very much like a tree, that are laid down between hibernation and active growth periods. Obviously this method is of no use in ascertaining a living hog's age!

Rule of thumb is to look at the colour of the spines. As a hog matures they change colour from black, grey and ivory to ginger, brown and ivory. After that it is purely guess work. The teeth will become worn down, although this could simply be a sign that the soil in their environment is gritty. The claws will look thicker and blunted as they mature. A really old hog will start to lose pigmentation of the skin, so a hog with pink-tinged nose and ears will be much older than one that is black. A hog in its first 18 months should have nice, white, new-looking teeth. A build-up of deposits, or worn teeth, especially at the back of the mouth are a good indication of age 3 years onwards.

The average life expectancy of a hog in the wild is between 3 to 5 years, however, hogs have been known to live till 7 or 8 years depending on their environment. In the last couple of years I have seen an increasing number of geriatric hogs being brought in for care, surely an indication of a good thriving population in the location they came from.

Handling of hogs will eventually give you experience and confidence to make a good guess at age deduction. It might be easiest to class them in one of the following five categories rather than guessing the actual years and months:

Baby: under 200 gm; should still be on mother's milk

Youth: on solids but still with mother

Juvenile: 350 gm upwards; not old enough to mate; big enough to be on own

Adult: usually 600 gm or over; of mating age

Geriatric: on its last season, worn teeth, pigmentation loss

It is important to compile some kind of record or chart for each hog in care which allows you easy reference to its progress, such as that on the following page.

Once you have noted the weight of the hog on admission, you record its weight over three days. This will tell you what weight value to use as a starting point on the vertical axis of the graph. Then put higher values on the vertical axis at 10 gm intervals. So, for example, if your starting point is 210 gm, put 220, 230, 240 etc. You may have to make another vertical axis at another place on the graph at, say, day 10 with a different set of values if its weight rises above, or falls below the set of values you made on day 1.

Date   Name of finder   Phone no.

Weight on admission		Male/Female		Age	

Eyes		Ears		Mouth	
Belly		Skirt		Limbs	
Armpit/Groin				Faeces	
Warm/Cold				**CHECKLIST**	

Day 2

Day 3

Notes

Weight chart

| Weight (g) | 1 | 2 | 3 | 4 | 5 | 6 | 7 | 8 | 9 | 10 | 11 | 12 | 13 | 14 Days |

Problem solving

The following pages describe common problems that occur with hedgehogs, together with solutions that I have found work well. The idea is to mix and match the solutions that suit best. A hog might be admitted cold and emaciated. It obviously will want warming up and given fluids. However, this is rarely what is actually wrong with it; these problems are often the result of an underlying problem. No hog will consciously starve itself without good reason.

The trick is to look beyond the obvious. A hog that has, for example, been attacked by a dog could have other problems. It might have been out during the day because it is struggling to find food due to an additional problem. Always keep an open mind. Remember you are not qualified to give a diagnosis to a second person; you can give an impression of what you think its problems are but leave the final diagnosis to a vet.

When handling a hog, ensure you are wearing latex gloves. They will protect you from possible ringworm which many hogs carry. This is a fungal infection and although nothing to worry about, and is easily cured, is best to guard against. Hogs also tend to carry salmonella in their gut, another reason for good hygiene. There is also the psychological reassurance that any fleas, ticks, mites, blood, pus, maggots etc will not come into contact with your flesh. And yes, the spines do hurt! They can leave you with minute scratches just breaking the surface of the skin, which are itchy and uncomfortable.

Strict hygiene is essential to protect yourself, your family and the other hogs in your care. Even when wearing gloves, wash your hands with antibacterial soap at the end of the session and with *Milton* between the handling of each hog. Do not use any utensils for hogs that will later be used in the kitchen. Invest in digital kitchen scales, small tubs for storing food and liquids, together with dishes for feeding and jugs for measuring.

1. How do I know if it needs help?

Any hog out during daylight hours can be classed as being in distress. They are nocturnal and should only surface under cover of darkness. Hogs out during the day could be desperate for food, or so cold they are trying to warm up—signs of obvious health problems. Occasionally a mother hog might be seen having a quick feed before going back to her babies, but this is so rare it is worth taking the gamble of bringing it in for a check-up. It can easily be returned to where it came from if nothing wrong can be found. Make a decision within 24 hours when dealing with a female (**No. 42**) in the summer months to minimise distress to any babies she may be looking after.

2. How do I pick it up?

Either put on some gardening gloves and carefully place your hands either side of the hog and lift it into a container, or throw a towel over it and gently push the hog so it becomes wrapped in the cloth, you can then easily pick it up. A hog that is relaxed - perhaps you have been treating it for a few days - can be 'scruffed' rather like a kitten being carried by its mother. If you choose this method ensure you are not simply grabbing the spines, you must have a good grasp of the flesh beneath and give support by placing the other hand under the hog. This only works if the hog's spines are laying flat on its body.

3. I have put it in a box with sawdust, covered it with grass and leaves and put it in the garage

Grass and dead leaves are not a good idea as they tend to be wet and will reduce a hog's body temperature further if it is already hypothermic. It could also infect any wounds that might be present and hide any faeces samples that may be deposited. Sawdust resembles fly eggs, so you will find it hard to differentiate between the two. Placing the box on a cold, concrete floor is not a good idea as it will speed up hypothermia due to heat loss through the bottom of the box, thus pushing a hog into a possible irreversible state. It is better to cover the hog with a towel and bring it into your utility room or house.

Any fleas it may have will not infest your house, dog or cat as they are classed as host specific. You might get bitten by a rogue flea but they cannot live on anything other than the hog.

Please don't be tempted to use cat or dog flea spray on the animal as it may be toxic to hogs. *Johnson's Rid-Mite* spray for birds (pyrethrum based) is the quickest, safest, and most efficient way of dealing with any possible fleas. This can be purchased in any pet shop. Another product that can be safely used is *Frontline*, available from your vet on prescription.

4. How should I contain it?

If you do not have an old rabbit hutch you could use a cat carrier or a large storage box. The box will have to be at least 35 cm high. Only use towels for bedding, as the amount of straw required for the hog to build a warm nest may allow it to climb on top and escape.

5. Cold to touch and won't uncurl

When a hog is deeply distressed it will curl up in defence. If it is also cold this exacerbates the situation. When handling the hog, after a minute or two you should be able to feel its body temperature through your gloves. Gently push your finger under its curled head and towards its tummy or feel for the gums to get a very quick indication of how cold it is. Place it either on a heat pad suitable for pets, under a basking lamp or on a hot-water bottle or plastic bottle filled with hot water. Ensure the water used is not so hot that it will burn the hog. There should also be sufficient space in the enclosure for the hog to move away from the heat source if it becomes too hot. Be aware that the last two options will quickly lose heat and will start to draw warmth away from the hog. You will have to be vigilant in making sure this situation does not occur. Ensure it is not directly in contact with the heat by wrapping a towel around the heat source. Place a small towel over the hog and leave it for about a half hour. It should show signs of uncurling after this time. Leave for another half hour and then check every ten minutes, turning the hog over from side to side to help distribute the heat evenly through the body. The hog may require constant warmth, even after it has initially warmed up. After the heat source has been removed, check it regularly to ensure that it does not deteriorate.

6. How do I get it to uncurl?

Once you have mastered this little trick you will be well on your way to handling hogs efficiently. Assuming the hog is not hypothermic, in which case start with **No.5**, the gentlest way is as follows. You have to discipline yourself to make no noise; the tuts and clicks and sighs we make to reassure domestic animals will be of no use here as they will cause the hog to curl up even tighter.

1. Place a towel over the worktable. The hog's spines dig into the towel which helps to keep the hog in position in step 6.

2. Hold the hog with both hands, the head end resting on the fingers of your left hand and the hind end on the fingers of your right hand, underbelly facing down (**Figure 1**).

3. With the hog and your hands still in this position, raise the hog upwards, just enough to cancel the effect of gravity, and not too fast so that it feels it could be in control of the situation if it were to uncurl.

4. Once it has taken the initiative and has placed all four feet on your hands, feel for its snout with two fingers of your left hand.

5. Place your left thumb on the back of its neck and your right thumb on the base of its spine.

6. Now comes the tricky bit. Flip the hog over very quickly onto its back and place it immediately on top of the towel (**Figure 2**).

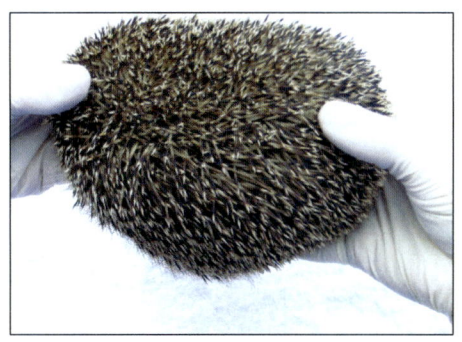

Figure 1

Figure 2

Figure 3

Figure 4

7. Slowly move your hands and fingers into a position that is comfortable to work with. It might decide to curl up again but do not let go of its snout.

8. With your free hand, 'walk' your fingers along the spines of its back, starting from its tail to the middle of its body (**Figure 3**).

9. It may take a little while but it should eventually relax enough for you to slowly tilt its head backwards.

10. Use the thumb nail of your left hand to find the front tooth in its upper jaw. Hold its head in place gently but firmly; don't try and force the hog open (**Figure 4**).

11. As the hog slightly relaxes take up the slack to prevent it curling back up. You should now have a prostrate hog on your table.

   It is a difficult process to explain and you will probably be left scratching your head in confusion, but it does make sense if you take it slowly!

7. Clump of spines return slowly after being pulled upwards

This is not unusual in a dehydrated hog. Do not give fluids to a cold animal; there is the possibility of inhalation pneumonia because a hog is unable to swallow when in this vulnerable condition. Follow **No.5** until it uncurls and then offer fluids, which should be given at body temperature or a little higher. Never give cold fluids to a cold hog. If it will lap from a shallow bowl then go with that. If it will not, you will have to pipette straight into the mouth. The best fluids to give are *Lectade*. Personally, I find these expensive and not easily obtainable as they can only be purchased from a vet. *Blackcurrant Dioralyte* or a pharmacy's own brand work just as well. You could even make up your own rehydration solution, which consists of:

- 1 litre of warm water
- 1 tablespoon of honey or sugar
- 1 teaspoon of salt

Try flavouring with blackcurrant juice to make more palatable.

Either insert a pipette into the hog's mouth between its front teeth or gently to the side of the mouth where the teeth are smallest. Use your thumbnail to coax the jaw open on the opposite side. The first few attempts to get it to swallow might not work. Persevere and it should eventually start to gulp down the solution. Tilting the head till you can peer down its mouth to the back of the throat encourages swallowing.

Patience is the answer to this one. Repeat this every half hour for a couple of hours giving a couple of millilitres each time and you should have a hog that is able to lap for itself. Subcutaneous fluids (those which are injected under the skin) are easy to administer and will help rehydrate a hog that for various reasons may not be possible to rehydrate orally. These are available from your vet, who will explain the procedure.

8. It is covered in fleas, mites or ticks

A hog infested with parasites usually has a further underlying problem. First, though, you need to rid the animal of this additional burden. Flea anaemia can be detected by looking at the hog's gums. They should be pink and if pressed gently the gums should change colour to white and then back to pink within two seconds. An anaemic hog will have white gums that do not change under pressure. Look at the base of the spines. If they appear to have a rusty coating along the shaft then it is quite likely that you need to de-flea it.

Hog fleas cannot live on your cat or dog and will not infest your house. However, some pets may have sensitive skin which could become irritated by being bitten by these parasites. One of the safest methods for flea eradication is *Johnson's Rid-Mite for birds*. It is a pyrethrum-based spray that is safe to use on hogs. Cat and dog sprays can be toxic and should never be used. A quick burst of a split-second over the back of the hog and one on either side should suffice. Cover the face of the hog with a cloth or your hand and give a very careful split-second spray to the underbelly. Leave for about 30 seconds and you should see the satisfying sight of all the spines moving involuntarily as the fleas die and fall out.

Mites can be detected as a fine white powder, usually amongst the fur of the hog, be it the underbelly, the skirt or the face. Strict hygiene should be exercised to prevent cross contamination with other hogs. With careful and close examination you should be able to see the powder moving. A microscope with a x2 magnifier is useful in the detection of this parasite, although cheap reading glasses should magnify things sufficiently to confirm infestation. Again, *Johnson's Rid-Mite* is a good eradicator. Spray around the skirt and the underbelly as previously instructed. In addition, spray a little of the chemical onto a small dish, and with a cotton bud absorb the liquid and wipe around the face if there is evidence of parasites there.

The hog should not be given straw bedding as it can take a little while to completely cure this problem and you ideally want bedding that is disposable. The nest should consist of a towel, with newspaper on the floor of the cage. The towel and paper should be removed and discarded and its environment disinfected with *Milton* on a daily basis.

Giving the hog a bath with *HiBiscrub* the following day should flush out the dead mites and remove any dead skin that has formed from the parasites. One part *HiBiscrub* to 20 parts water in a container big enough to hold the hog should suffice. Give the hog a soak for a few minutes and agitate a little by lifting it out and putting it back into the water. It should uncurl, thus enabling you to get your fingers onto its underbelly and give a little rub. Wrap it loosely in a towel and put it back to bed. It might be worth giving it a heat source so it can get fully warmed up after its bath.

Repeat the whole process after about five days. If you still see mites crawling around, refer the hog to your vet for treatment. Although not licensed, *Stronghold* or *Advocate* for small cats drizzled on the back of the hog's neck has proved very effective. This drug is only obtainable from your vet.

Ticks are related to spiders and crawl around just as easily. They gorge on blood, turning black in the process before falling off into the hog's nest. They travel from one hog to another through the hog's habit of sharing nests. They are attracted to carbon dioxide and so a sick hog resting up for long periods is a sitting target for a tick.

These parasites bury their head into the hog and start feeding on its blood. In general, the longer the hog has been ill the more ticks it will have. If this parasite is removed inefficiently it could inject a toxic substance into the hog that will make the hog ill. Also leaving the tick's head embedded in the skin can lead to infections, so an efficient removal method is required.

By far the easiest and quickest is to use a *tick-removing gadget* purchased from your vet or pet shop. This comprises a handle with an angled fork at the end. You simply slide the fork under the tick, turn it clockwise a couple of times and then gently pull outwards. The tick is then removed, complete with head.

Ticks are usually situated amongst the spines, around and in the ears, around the neck, along the skirt, down the legs and around the tail and hind-quarters. The largest are usually at the front of the hog, the smallest around the tail. If there is a massive infestation that you feel will take a long time to remove, then pace yourself. Remember you have a wild animal in your hands that is not well and will be feeling very vulnerable and distressed.

Check the back first and carefully remove any tick that is easily accessible. Move on to the face, ears and skirt and finally the underbelly. You could concentrate on the white ticks as the darker ones will soon fall off into the nest. The nest should consist of a towel and newspaper on the floor of the cage. As with the mite infestation, change this daily. Be very careful when you come to remove ticks from the underbelly; both male and female hogs have two rows of nipples running either side of their belly from just below the armpits to just in front of the hind legs. These nipples are small and black and look remarkably like ticks!

9. What are the orange patches on its body?

A small, raised orange patch on the body or face of a hog could be harvest mites. These can be easily eradicated using *Johnson's Rid-Mite*. Simply spray a small amount onto a dish and absorb a little of the liquid onto a cotton bud. Gently rub this onto the orange patch. If there are still mites present after five days, repeat the process.

10. Why do hogs have a reputation for being covered in fleas?

If you can easily see fleas on a hog then it is, in all probability, staying out during the day. This is not normal behaviour for a hog and suggests it is experiencing difficulties. That being the case, it is not uncommon for its parasite burden to increase dramatically, thus fuelling the myth of hogs being infested with fleas.

11. Appears to be sawdust in and around the eyes

Hogs found in distress during the summer months are in real danger of myiasis or fly strike (the laying of eggs onto a sick animal by blue or green-bottle flies), which will quickly hatch into maggots. A common place for flies to lay their eggs is inside the eye socket and anywhere on the body where it might be damp, such as armpits or groin. If the eggs are on the body or around the eye, carefully comb them out in a flicking motion using tweezers or a cocktail stick. If the fur is dry where the eggs have been laid, it is a relatively easy job to complete. The remaining eggs can be picked out with tweezers.

I have observed that when a hog is warmed up and it reaches optimum body temperature, the eggs do not appear to be viable and simply fall from the animal's body. This is not a 100 % guaranteed situation, so remove all of the eggs manually. If eggs are in the eye socket, then carefully open it using finger and thumb at the top and bottom of the eye. With a clean pipette filled with *Optrex*, flush the eye socket so that the eggs simply float out. Repeat this several times until you are sure you have removed all the eggs.

A word of caution regarding equipment placed close to the animal's eyes. Hold whatever you are using side-on to its eyeball so that if the animal does its characteristic 'jump' in defence, you are less likely to scratch its eye.

12. Thick, ivory-coloured clumps over the face, hind-quarters and skirt

This is indicative of myiasis and is very easily remedied in the same way as around the eye; see **No.11**.

13. Maggots crawling in the eye socket

Very distressing to witness but easily remedied. It does not follow that the hog will necessarily lose its sight. Open the eye (as in **No.11**), remove any escaping maggots with tweezers and flush out any remaining maggots with *Optrex*. If you decide to use a cotton bud to remove excess fluid, ensure the cotton bud is damp. Never use dry absorbent material directly on the eyeball as it can easily scratch the delicate surface.

Great care should be taken regarding the protection of your own eyesight during this process. Hogs have a tendency to 'jump' or 'hic-cup' in an attempt to stab you with their spines, giving a startling huff at the same time. You will obviously be quite close to the animal while working on it so make sure at all times you angle any tools away from your face. It is very easy to become startled by their defensive action and poke yourself in the face with the end of the tool you are working with.

14. Maggots crawling from under its tail

Again, this is very distressing to witness. Flies will lay eggs just in or around the anus. What you are most likely seeing are the maggots crawling in and out from just inside the hog. It rarely means it has an intestinal tract full of the grubs. Firstly check for possible infested wounds that might be near the tail and then proceed with tweezers, removing the grubs as they appear.

15. One eye stays closed

Check that there is an eyeball in the socket and that it has not turned white, which would mean the eye is dead and beyond help, not uncommon in mature hogs. It may be due to an irritant, fly eggs for example, so flush with *Optrex*. If there is no sign of improvement within the next hour or two it may need *Fucithalmic eye ointment* (a prescription medicine requiring a veterinary appointment).

16. Cannot see its eyes

A hog that is very dehydrated can have deeply sunken eyes. When the lids are opened it can be extremely difficult to find the eyeballs. By placing your finger and thumb to top and bottom of the eyelids and gently opening the lids and moving them back towards the ear, you should hopefully expose the eyeball. Take this opportunity to check for fly eggs that might have been deposited into the sockets. Follow **No.7** for rehydration and **No.11** and **No.13** for removal of foreign bodies.

17. Appears to have black scabs over the eyes

If a hog gets a blow to the head, either one or both of the eyes may prolapse (pop out of their sockets). If it has happened that day, the eyes may still be moist. However, it is much more likely to have happened a few days before, in which case the eye will have become dry and dead, with what looks like a crusty scab covering it. Either way there is nothing that can be done regarding recovery of sight or returning the eye back into the head.

Use *Optrex* to gently bathe the eye and carefully remove any debris before having the condition confirmed by your vet. Smearing *Aloe Vera gel* onto the eyeball will help prevent flies from buzzing round. Repeat this every day until the eye finally shrivels up and sloughs off. The hog should now be able to close its eyelids. Check for infection each time you bathe the eyes. If pus starts to ooze from behind the eyeball, a course of antibiotics will be required, so seek veterinary help.

18.Open wound full of maggots

Maggots are not fussy; they may start by feeding on an open wound but will carry on into the hog's body, finally killing the animal. The hog might go into shock and require pain relief or antibiotics. If, therefore, it is the first time you have come across this type of injury it would be advisable to consult a vet who will guide you as to the best course of action.

It is a time-consuming exercise, but the best remedy I have found to get rid of maggots is to simply remove them, one by one, with tweezers. Look for a glistening movement on the hog's body rather than a maggot shape; it becomes a much quicker process and enables you to simply switch onto 'auto-pilot'. Start with those that are easy to remove and just work your way through. Don't be tempted to wash them out, it doesn't work. All you will achieve is getting the hog wet and its whole body will glisten as it dries out, thus masking the movement of the grubs.

Maggots are amazing things. Once they know they are under attack they will scatter and you will be left with an area devoid of grubs. Wait a few moments quietly and they should all start to return. You may have to repeat this process many times until you successfully remove them all. Bear in mind that you are working on a scared wild animal so remember to check that the hog is not getting too stressed. Even after you think you have caught the last grub, check every hour or so as there is always one that slips away. If you think there were more crawling around than you removed, then they may have moved to a second wound. Focus very carefully on the area you find the grub in. Sometimes there is nothing more than a small hole that the maggots have dived into, but that hole could contain many maggots. Hover over the hole with tweezers and watch for the glistening of the grub's skin as it crawls around. Give the wound a final flush with salt water to hopefully drive out any remaining maggots. If you find the hog scratching at one particular area over the next few hours or days check carefully that a rogue grub has not been left to cause damage.

19. A wound beneath the spines I cannot get to

With small scissors carefully snip away the spines that are obscuring the wound. Also remove the spines around the very edge as they are prone to falling into the wound and sticking to the damaged flesh.

Wear glasses to protect your eyes as the spines tend to ping in all directions. Note that hogs shed their spines in a random fashion over many months, growing new ones on a continual basis, very much like the hair on your head. A missing spine will be replaced quickly once the wound has healed, but a spine that has been clipped could stay with the hog for up to 12 months as its body does not know the spine has been damaged. Therefore clip as few spines as possible, just enough to reach the damaged area, or you could have a recovered hog that cannot be released for many months after the initial problem has been rectified due to a vulnerable bald patch.

20. How do I treat open wounds?

Once you have access to the damaged area (**No.19**), remove any debris with tweezers and drizzle diluted *HiBiscrub*, one part *HiBiscrub* to 20 parts water, onto the wound. Only a small amount will be required, about an egg-cup full.

With a cotton bud, gently wipe the area to remove dirt and grit. The course of action you take will depend on the depth of the wound. A surface wound can be flushed daily with the same solution of *HiBiscrub* until the area has healed. Exposing the area for about 15 minutes at a time to the sun and air is beneficial as it dries out the environment that the bacteria thrive in, thus speeding healing. You need to have a trusting hog for this, though, as the last thing you want to do is stress it further.

A deep, or puncture wound, is prone to turning into an abscess or becoming infected. This will need to be kept open and flushed out daily. If a scab forms over the wound it might trap bacteria and cause an abscess which may track inside the body causing more infection. Antibiotics are essential, so veterinary treatment will be required. Certainly presenting the vet with a clean wound makes treatment much quicker and the vet will be able to see at a glance what is going on.

21. A large lump or swelling

It could be one of several problems, the most likely being an abscess. This will require lancing and the abscess should be kept open and flushed out daily. Abscesses are notorious for tracking under the skin in hogs, sometimes getting into the bones and infecting them or causing septicaemia, at which point there is little that can be done for the animal. If the abscess has burst it can be flushed out with diluted *HiBiscrub*; see **No.20**.

Once you have removed as much pus as possible try using *Hydrogen Peroxide 6 %*. Dilute 1 part *Hydrogen Peroxide* to about 20 parts water. Place your finger in the solution. If it fizzes slightly around the edges of your nail it is at the correct dilution. Use this to give a final flush of the wound. The fizzing action forces oxygen deep into the wound, flushing out any remaining pus, killing the bacteria, which do not survive in an oxygen-rich environment, and destroying organic matter that might clog up the wound. I have seen amazing results with this method. Repeat twice a day, and with the help of antibiotics you should be well on the way to a positive result.

If a hog arrives with a suspected abscess, but you are unable to get a vet appointment that day, the pressure can be alleviated by inserting a wide bore canula into the swelling and drawing off any pus that might be there. The hypodermic should fill with ivory coloured liquid, thus confirming your suspicions. This is, however, a very temporary solution because without opening the site, administering antibiotics and flushing the wound out, it will only fill with pus again and get steadily worse. Do not proceed with this method unless you have already been shown how by a vet. It is easy to go in too deep and puncture lungs or intestines thus causing further, more serious problems.

Tumour growths are also a possibility and can be seen in many forms. Veterinary diagnosis and treatment will be required. Hernias are also seen as lumps around the groin area. They occur when a tear in the abdominal wall allows a small part of the intestine to poke out. This will require surgery to push it back and will need to be secured with sutures.

Basically, any swelling should be referred to a vet. If you try opening a lump to see what is inside you may be doing more harm than good. As you will be requiring antibiotics anyway, it makes sense to leave all the work to the vet.

22. A wound on its face that coincides with where its claws rest when curled up, preventing healing

Tubigauze from pharmacies or supermarkets is ideal to pad out the offending limb and claws. Simply follow the instructions as for dressing a human finger. You might have to pad the claws or clip them (**No.23**), prior to dressing with the bandage to stop them poking through the cloth. Change the dressing regularly when it becomes dirty.

23. How short can I clip its claws?

It should not be necessary to clip a hog's claws as they are required to be long for grooming and foraging. However, if the hog has a damaged foot which has caused the claws to grow in an uneven fashion, just take the claw ends off with either small scissors suitable for nails, or pet nail clippers used for dogs' or cats' claws.

There is a living core to the nail that is difficult to detect, which if cut, will be extremely painful for the hog and will bleed profusely, so be careful to avoid this area.

24.One limb sticks out when it curls up

This is usually indicative of a damaged limb, though not necessarily broken. Carefully uncurl the hog (**No. 6**), and as gently as possible take the offending limb between your finger and thumb, exerting resistance to stop it curling back into its body. Hogs usually realise very quickly they have 'met their match' and will allow the limb to be fully extended. You can then check what is going on. If you can pull both matching limbs out together you will be able to compare like for like. If not, just go slowly.

Look for any obvious wounds. Has the leg been broken and reset itself? Is there anything trapped around it? Check to see if it is walking on its knuckles. Has the fur worn down in one area? Has hard skin formed or have claws grown in an uneven fashion? These are all signs of an old injury. It is best to seek veterinary advice for this as some injuries can be treated if seen quickly and anti-inflammatory drugs administered if necessary. Sometimes amputation is the only road to recovery.

Bear in mind that a hog with any missing limbs will not be releasable and will require an enclosed safe garden. Taking this further, a hog requires both front legs for balance, digging, climbing and righting itself if it falls over. I have had a hog that pulled its own front leg off to escape entrapment. I decided to follow through care as a fait accompli. He coped reasonably well for the 6 months he survived, but I felt uneasy when I saw him ambling laboriously around and would certainly not advocate amputation of front limbs. They can cope reasonably well with a hind leg being removed, but their ability to groom themselves is reduced by 50 %. When a hog wakes up at night it will systematically scratch itself from its neck, down its back in a grooming fashion, removing dead skin cells, fleas, ticks and old spines. A hog with a missing leg lays itself open to a build-up of parasites and possible skin problems, so extra attention will be needed for this animal.

Check its ear on the damaged side for mites (**No.8**). It may enjoy being regularly groomed with a scrubbing brush. Like cats and dogs, when you rub a point on their ear or back, they will lean into the scratching motion or even move their hind leg as if doing the scratching themselves.

25. Both hind legs remain outside the ball when it curls up

Check along its back. You may find the spines bristling at the front half of the body but lying flat at the rear. This means there has been some damage to the spinal column. Try pinching the toes on the back feet. If it reacts then there is obviously some feeling there and, after rest, the hog may possibly regain the use of its hind-quarters.

Getting no reaction to pinching the toes is not a good sign. You have two courses of action: give it a few days and see if it repairs itself, or take it to the vet for painkillers and anti-inflammatory drugs. Anti-inflammatory painkillers are best administered soon after the damage has occurred and may not prove as effective in an old injury. X-rays are an expense that you might not want to pursue.

Seven days of rest should see on improvement as long as it can drag itself to its food and water without causing itself damage. If not, the damage may be irreversible and it should be put to sleep. Also be aware it may require manual evacuation of bowels or bladder. Veterinary instruction should be sought here.

Another thing to look for that may tell you quickly if it is worth pursuing is the general condition of the animal. If it has sustained these injuries some time ago it will be very thin and dehydrated, a sign that in all probability the outcome will not be good. A hog in general good health indicates the injury has only just happened and treatment is worth pursuing. Be aware that a fractured pelvis can leave nerve damage to one or more of the hind legs, thus causing them to be dragged.

It has taken up to six weeks before signs of improvement have been seen in a hog with such problems. Veterinary advice was sought for such a hog on one occasion. No treatment other than good food and a safe environment was prescribed. His weight continued to gain, a good sign for any captive animal, and he was eventually able to use his legs sufficiently to be released.

26. Appears to have a broken jaw

Take the hog immediately to a vet. It is possible to wire a jaw if it is displaced, but quite often the damage is so old it cannot be repaired. Euthanasia may be the only course of action. For a simple fracture, liquidised food, anti-inflammatory painkillers and antibiotics should remedy the problem.

27. Won't close its mouth and sounds as if it is having difficulty breathing

Probably snout or jaw injury. Either way if it is unable to swallow it will be dehydrated. Veterinary guidance should be sought, either to show how to give subcutaneous fluids with the addition of anti-inflammatory painkillers if appropriate, or for re-wiring of the jaw, or euthanasia.

28. It needs to be anaesthetised by a vet—do I starve it first?

Hogs have a very fast metabolism and so starving them for any time is never a good idea and not necessary prior to anaesthetic.

29. Appears someone has taken scissors and snipped spines off at random

Indicative of an attack. A dog, fox or badger will roll the animal over to try and penetrate the spines, breaking some in the process. Badgers are the hog's main predator and are well adapted to uncurling hogs with their long claws. The first encounter a hog has with this predator is usually its last! Jack Russells are keen to attack hogs, often sustaining very painful injuries to themselves in the process. Other tell-tale signs of an attack are limbs that don't retract into the ball and crush injuries to the snout. Sometimes you will find mud caked into their snout or feet due to being pushed into the ground. Puncture wounds and tearing of the skin are also signs of an attack.

Look for two sets of puncture wounds, one from the upper jaw and one from the lower jaw of the attacker. Limbs may be broken and abscesses present due to the penetration of the teeth into the hog's body. Antibiotics will be required to clear up any infection together with pain relief if appropriate. Treat the wounds as for **No.19** and **No.20** before taking the hog to the vet. If traumatised by the attack, a hog may try to kick out with its legs or bite you; this is the only time I have experienced this behaviour in a hog.

I have already mentioned dog and fox attacks, but the same is true for cruelty by humans. Try to be as quiet and gentle as possible in these cases. It might be best to leave it an hour in the warm to calm down before handling it. Keep it in the dark and give it a towel to snuggle under. *Dioralyte* and a little food may help speed recovery. Certainly, as soon as it has taken food or water you will know it has started to calm down.

30. All the spines have gathered as a clump on the top of the body and the tail is sticking up

This is known as pop-off syndrome, named by Les Stocker, and is specific to hogs. If a hog has struggled severely in attempts to free itself, instead of its muscles pulling the spines under the body, they slip over the top exposing their hind limbs and hips. It looks very distressing, but does not appear to hurt the animal. The hog may require an anaesthetic and for the skin to be held firmly in place as it gains consciousness. Try warming the animal first, and offer it a calm environment to see if it sorts itself out. If there is no improvement within a few hours then seek veterinary treatment.

31.Feels light for its large size

Balloon syndrome (emphysema) is another distressing sight. This can be the result of either damage to the lung causing air to escape under the skin, or a puncture wound to the body causing gas-producing bacteria. Either way a vet is required.

32.Passing blood and vomiting

Quite possibly rat poisoning. *Charcoal* can be given in the early stages, together with *vitamin K*, which is a good specific antidote to poisons that cause clotting problems. Unfortunately, once poisons have been ingested and organs start to shut down, very little can be done to save the hog. Veterinary assistance should be sought immediately for possible euthanasia.

Hogs' foraging habits leave them wide open to consuming some very toxic substances, for example, slug pellets. Typical signs of this type of poisoning are anxiety, drooling, wobbling, trembling, occasionally bluish faeces and vomiting. There might be evidence of a blue deposit to the flanks of the hog as it self-anoints after consuming the poison. Hogs quite often by-pass the dead slugs and simply go straight for the pellets. One heaped teaspoon of slug pellets is sufficient to poison an adult hog.

33.Green, blood-stained faeces or dark diarrhoea

Quite often a hog has not been able to feed itself for some time due to health problems. Its first faeces may look like tar, quickly followed by a more solid-looking stool. Green or blood-stained faeces may return to normal after 12 hours on good food; any longer will require treatment. Rule of thumb, if it gains weight, allow good diet to remedy. Hogs tend to have a background burden of internal worms which show themselves as a green slimy end to the droppings. If weight falls and this type of dropping is evident, use *Panacur 10 %* liquid wormer, 1 drop per 100 gm of body weight over 10 days, to a maximum of 4 drops daily, either in its food or directly into its mouth. Try diluting with *water* or *Dioralyte* if you are administering straight into its mouth, otherwise put it in a little food, withholding its main meal until it has eaten the medicated batch.

You are not looking to completely eradicate the burden, only to reduce it to a more manageable level. The continued occurrence of blood or totally green, jelly-like faeces after 24 hours will require antibiotics. Take a sample with you to the vet for visual analysis.

34. Appears to be passing worms in its faeces

Sinewy faeces are a sign of severe intestinal breakdown. What you are seeing is the passing of gut lining. Good rehydration fluids are essential. Failure to gain weight or no change in motions within 12 hours requires veterinary intervention in the form of antibiotics. Take a sample with you.

35. Nose is continually dripping and it is coughing

Hogs naturally have a wet nose. However, excessive dripping could be indicative of pneumonia or lungworm infestation. Hold the hog—can you feel a rattling sound as it breaths in and out?

Hogs tend to harbour lungworm and seem prone to pneumonia in the wild. Treatment for both is the same as it can be hard to differentiate between the two. A course of 4 drugs is required with a total of 12 injections: a steroid to help reduce inflammation in the lungs; a drug to kill the worms; a drug to stimulate coughing to rid the lung of debris; and antibiotics to combat infection. Again, veterinary treatment is required.

36.Fur missing from face, dry flaky skin, base of some spines look rotten, skin infected, skin around skirt cracked and bleeding

Your hog might only show a few of these symptoms, depending on the severity. Most hogs harbour ringworm. Sometimes this gets out of control, perhaps due to another problem the hog is experiencing, which lowers its immune system. If the problem becomes very severe, spines will start to fall out.

In mild cases offer good quality food as previously mentioned (**Basic care for hogs in captivity, page 10**). Quite often this is all that is required to enable the hog to build itself up. Signs of improvement should be evident after about 5 days.

To test for ringworm you will need to purchase from your vet a culture-growing Petri dish, and to take skin scrapings or pluck a hair from the affected part of the body. Don't use spines as they tend to harbour all sorts of bacteria that may interfere with the culture growth.

Sprinkle the skin scraping onto the jelly and leave for 5 to 10 days. The culture should turn a lovely cherry red if it is positive; you then give two baths, 10 days apart, of *Imaverol*. You will first have to book an appointment with your vet to get this medication. Take the culture growth to the vet for diagnosis. Be aware, however, that non-reaction in the Petri dish does not necessarily mean it is not ringworm. You may have to repeat the test.

If the hog's skin becomes dry and cracked around the skirt, a little *Aloe Vera gel* + *vitamin E* (obtainable from supermarkets) or *Tea-tree ointment* or *99.9 % Aloe Vera gel* (Holland & Barrett) are all good products to lubricate and soften this area, thus enabling the animal to move more comfortably.

Be aware that UV light will not fluoresce hog ringworm, a method of detection commonly used for fungal infection in other animals. Also be very careful not to catch this yourself or pass it on to other hogs. Wear protective gloves, handle this hog last, and wash all utensils thoroughly with *Milton*.

37. Will not eat given food

Hogs can be surprisingly fussy for a wild animal that scavenges and eats bugs for a living. Because the animal is sick, it should be catered for. I use good quality chicken cat food in jelly and *Spike's World dried food*. A hog would naturally take in fibre from the exoskeletons of the insects it eats, so add a *Weetabix*, or equivalent, to the tinned food as a substitute. Use one *Weetabix* to one tin of food; add 1 pinch of *SA37* per hog and you should then have a very palatable meal. *Iams* dried chicken cat food is very well received by most hogs, even those with few teeth. *Cooked chicken* portions broken up may encourage a fussy animal to start eating, especially if the food is still warm. Liquidised tinned food with added *water* or *Dioralyte* may encourage a hog to lap.

I have had limited success with cooked and raw eggs, mashed bananas, cooked potato, chicken Complan, meal worms, digestive and rich tea biscuits and dog food, although many carers swear that their animals love all or some of these.

The only hogs I successfully hand-feed are babies or hogs that have difficulties getting to food and water, due to, for example, extreme emaciation and dehydration, damaged limbs, recent loss of sight or a blow to the head resulting in disorientation. All of these problems are very quickly overcome by the hog and certainly within 24 hours they should be making some effort to feed themselves.

Those capable of feeding, but for unknown reasons choose not to, usually fail to survive. Hand-feeding tends to cause more problems as most will vomit what they have taken in, thus stressing the hog and exacerbating the dehydration that it is inevitably suffering from. On every occasion that I have tried hand-feeding an anorexic hog it has always resulted in a steady decline in the animal followed by death. There is obviously more going on than I have been able to identify. Even with veterinary intervention the end is usually death.

38. Flies lay eggs in the food bowls

Give dried food during the day and then in the late evening add the tinned food. First thing in the morning discard any food left in the bowl and put fresh dried food out again. This works well with most hogs. You may encounter a hog that will only eat tinned food. In this case, if it is in a cage or hutch, cover the cage with curtain netting to prevent flies gaining access. This is also a good idea if you have a hog with open wounds which are attracting flies. Otherwise you will simply have to continually put small amounts of food out and clean the bowl regularly throughout the day.

39. What food will encourage hogs into my garden?

The simplest food is *Spike's World dried food*, or *dried chicken cat or dog food*. Use a good quality food as the cheaper products tend to have fish added which hogs are unable to digest. Crushed peanuts for birds are also welcomed by most hogs. Whatever you use, leave it under a feeding station which can simply consist of two bricks with a piece of wood across the top. Throw the food underneath the wood, which should discourage cats but allow hogs to easily reach what is on offer. If cats are a problem you could just use crushed peanuts. Tinned chicken cat or dog food can be used, but you will be left with a mucky bowl to clean out each day that will possibly attract flies.

Never give milk or bread as they can cause diarrhoea which, in a small animal, can prove fatal. You will know if a hog has found the food as they eat the food where they find it, leaving crumbs behind at the end of the meal. Mice, rats and squirrels all take the food away to eat and so will usually leave a clean bowl apart from their small droppings.

40. Where should a nest box be positioned?

The ideal place would be under a shrub or prickly bush, away from any busy part of the garden.

41. Will not stop pacing

A hog deeply stressed or which has recently lost its sight might frantically try to escape and pace in a hyperactive fashion. If it has a straw nest, give extra straw, or if a towel, add torn and screwed-up newspaper so it can add these to its nest. Check the hog is not too hot and cover the enclosure so that it is in the dark. Try scattering dried food on the enclosure floor to encourage foraging.

Try one method at a time, giving at least a half-hour between each distraction. You should have a calmer hog at the end of this time. Once it has calmed down be very careful how you approach its enclosure and do not clean out or disturb any more than is necessary.

I have on a very few occasions been met with a hog that, although thin and with no visible difficulties or ailments, continued to pace for hours at a time. I decided it was doing itself too much harm in relation to the care that was required and that the only course of action was to release it into a secure garden. The animal is then in an environment it feels more at home with and is being cared for at a distance simply by the provision of food and a quiet recovery site.

42.Is it male or female?

Very easy to differentiate. When hogs are born all their 'bits and pieces' are grouped by the tail. As they develop, a male's 'bits' move away from the tail eventually stopping around its belly. When a male curls up slightly you will be able to observe its penis on its belly just below where its nose rests. Therefore, a hog with what appears to be a belly button is in fact a male.

43.A female has started gathering nesting material and is not eating

A female hog that is in captivity during late spring to late summer could be pregnant. The first sign you may have of this is that she suddenly stops feeding or she tears up paper to add to the nest. Offer more nesting material. A mother that is stressed or which has had its nest disturbed shortly after giving birth may destroy the babies, so be extremely careful about how you approach the nest for the next few days. If her health problem is not life-threatening, consider not disturbing her for a few days. Baby hogs can be successfully hand-reared from about 5 days old, so if she were to abandon them at this stage you could step in and help.

44.White sticky substance on the male underbelly

When a male hog becomes stressed it may ejaculate. This is probably no more than sperm. Keep the animal in a quiet environment.

45.Male has small puncture wounds on its underbelly

Usually associated with being on the thin side. This could just be a very active male that has mounted many females and incurred damage to its belly from her spines. Check for fly eggs and maggots

(**No.11**, **No.12**, **No.13** and **No.14**) and keep him for a few days until the wounds have healed and he has gained weight.

46. Flies keep laying eggs on the sick hog

Prevent the flies from gaining access by keeping the hog in a cage or hutch that you can cover tightly with curtain netting.

47. Sick adult in the breeding season

Always a difficult one. If it is a female and you can see nothing wrong with it and it appears to be of a good weight and moving easily, you could consider letting her go back where she came from. Obvious injuries will have to be taken into account.

If you decide to keep her, listen out for possible distressed babies. They are very vociferous and cheep rather like a budgie or sparrow with attitude. It might be worth dropping a note to the immediate neighbours to where the hog was found just in case a nest is in their garden.

If it is a male, the decision is easier to make. It will do no harm to keep it overnight. If all seems well, it can be released the next evening. Hogs that appear to have nothing wrong with them do not take kindly to being in captivity; they tend not to settle and will possibly lose weight overnight in their quest to escape, so bear that in mind when you check it the next day. If it moves well, has a good covering of body fat and its faeces look normal, then you have covered most eventualities and it should be alright to release back to where it came from.

48. A mother and babies have been brought in for care—what should I do?

Handle them as little as possible and place in a large enclosure. If they came in a cardboard box, simply cut a hole big enough for mum to get out and place directly into the enclosure. If necessary, cover the box with an old plastic compost bag to prevent it from disintegrating in the rain. Clean the bowls daily and offer clean straw but do not be tempted to disturb the nest. With any luck, mum will continue to look after the babies. Alternatively, you could simply place a box with a hole cut into it under a shrub in your garden and follow **No.50** and **No.62.**

49. What takes priority, the mother or the babies?

If an adult female hog that is in care requires treatment, or it is in danger of dying, then it should have priority over its babies. If faced with the situation where a hog gives birth in captivity but has, for example, maggot-infested wounds, then at the risk of her abandoning her babies, the mother must obviously have priority treatment.

50. How do I move a nest located in an inconvenient place?

Firstly, is it really necessary to disturb the nest? The mother may move her babies of her own accord after a few weeks. Certainly at about 8 weeks they should be independent enough to make their own way in the world.

If you really have to move them, wear gloves. Prepare a cardboard box as for **No.62.** Leave the back open, then quickly pick up the nest and carefully place it in the box with mother and babies. Fasten the back of the box with tape and place the box under a shrub or behind a shed. Cover the entire box and the front entrance with an old plastic compost bag fastened to the ground with tent pegs. Offer a little dried food near the entrance of the box to encourage mum to stay, and then leave well alone.

If mum does abandon the babies you will soon know by the loud cheeping noise they make; you will then have to hand-rear them. The mum might decide to move them from the box back to the original nest, so ensure you have not left her original nest site in situ. After being moved, the mum might kill the babies, so please do not move a nest unless there is absolutely no alternative.

51. Accidentally uncovered a nest—what should I do?

Do not handle the babies. Quickly cover the nest up and leave well alone. The same scenarios apply to this situation as in **No.48** and **No.50**. Do not move the nest. Simply offer some food to encourage mum to stay around and listen out over the next couple of days for possible distressed babies.

52. Fallen down a hole and I cannot get it out

Use a pair of pliers to grab the spines at one end of the hog, and another pair of pliers to grab the spines at the other end of the hog, and gently but firmly, pull upwards. The more spines you can get hold of, the less discomfort for the hog.

The condition of the animal will decide what course of action to take once it is out. Certainly it will do no harm to keep it for a couple of days on a good diet just to ensure it has sustained no hidden injuries.

53. Fallen into pond

This animal will quite probably be cold and hypothermic. Follow **No.5**. There will probably be nothing visibly wrong with it, but check. The next problem is how long you should keep it. If it has inhaled the pond water, inhalation pneumonia is a real possibility. You will have to keep it for about 3 days to see if this occurs. Signs will be laboured, crackly breathing. Veterinary treatment will be required in the form of steroids and antibiotics.

54. How do I ensure hogs can escape from my pond?

Hogs are good swimmers. The problem arises when they fall into a pond with steep sides which they are unable to climb out of. If you are at the design stage of your pond, ensure it has a shallow edge. This will also encourage birds to use it as a bathing area. Place plants all around the edge to form a 'carpet' for the hog to climb onto. If it is an established pond, a ladder of chicken wire could be placed against the side of the pond and moulded into shape to be unobtrusive, or place a small wooden ramp on the edge leading into the water.

55. Tangled in netting

Remove the net by cutting it away with scissors if necessary. This should be done quickly, quietly and efficiently to reduce further stress to the animal. The netting may be restricting the hog's breathing, so speed is of the essence. When you have finished, check around its limbs and neck to ensure that you have not missed any netting that may still be cutting into the hog. Keep it for about 3 days to enable any injuries to appear. Restriction in blood supply could result in the animal losing limbs or sloughing off skin. It will probably be very stiff and aching from exertion, so a little bed-rest will do it no harm.

56. Trapped in garage/outbuilding

It will require rehydration in the form of *Dioralyte* or similar, followed by good quality food. Check its claws which may be worn down due to frantic digging attempts to escape. Don't release it until the claws have grown back sufficiently to enable it to forage successfully.

57. Sunbathing in garden

Hogs are nocturnal. If a hog is laying in the sun it is quite possibly suffering from hypothermia and desperately trying to warm up. Proceed with **No.5** and check for fly eggs and maggots (**No.11, No.12, No.13** and **No.14**).

58. Hibernating in the open

Hogs will not hibernate anywhere that is not completely secure and private. Their nests are similar to mice nests which are usually made beneath a structure such as a shed, or in brambles. Any hog in an apparent hibernating state in the open is in serious difficulties. **No.5** should be referred to first, followed by any other relevant solutions to problems that arise.

59. Is it hibernating or dead?

Not as daft as it sounds. A hog, when hibernating, still has the reflex ability to bristle its spines in a sweeping fashion, swelling in size and quite often emitting a loud bellows-like sound. If in doubt follow **No.5.** If it is dead you will probably notice an unpleasant smell. If there is absolutely no movement after 24 hours you can safely assume it is dead.

60. I want to light a bonfire, but worried a hog may be hibernating in it

The only safe way is to remove part of the bonfire and immediately light it in the new location, continually feeding the fire from the main pile. There are always possible problems whatever time of the year. You could have babies nesting, adults sleeping or hibernating. It can take a few hours for a hibernating hog to wake up sufficiently to move away from the danger of a bonfire, by which time it will most probably have sustained serious injuries.

61. Can it be released with a limb or eye missing?

Hogs do survive in the wild with deformities such as broken and reset limbs or missing eyes. The problem is they are usually the hogs that are found with additional problems at a later date. For my own part I would not release animals that have a major disadvantage over other hogs; they have a hard enough time as it is without any additional handicaps. Nor would I keep them in a hutch or rabbit run; they would have to go into an enclosed secure garden.

If the hog is young and missing one eye, you could consider general release as it has the whole of its life ahead of it and it would be a waste to deprive it of freedom.

I tend to keep very old hogs with disabilities in as large an enclosure as they can cope with. Treat each animal as an individual and cater for its personal needs rather than tying yourself down to a rule cut in stone.

The only true gardens that I have successfully used for non-releasable hogs have been those enclosed by a brick wall. Even gardens whose fences rest on concrete gravel boards sunk into the ground are not usually sufficient to keep a hog in; they just scratch away at the soil to create an escape route.

62. Have nursed it back to health, what should I do next?

A hog should weigh about 450 gm in the summer and up to 600 gm in the autumn if it is that year's offspring; an older hog will probably weigh more. Look at its body shape—it should be very plump and round when curled up. I don't tend to release hogs after November but keep them over the winter. Don't release hogs the week before or after Bonfire night for obvious reasons.

If you are in contact with the finder, see if they are happy for it to be released back into their garden if that was where it was found. It is always best to re-introduce hogs back to the area where they were found.

Stress that this is not a pet. It contravenes the Wildlife Act to catch a wild animal and keep it captive, and in most cases it is cruel. You could point out that diseases such as ringworm and salmonella can be caught without proper hygiene, a very good way of distancing the recipient from the hog! Reassure them of the host-specific flea, always a worry when they have dogs and cats.

I personally would not release a hog into a garden if they have a Jack Russell or similar 'ratting' dog. I have lost count of the number of animals brought in due to Jack Russell attacks. Check that no slug pellets or rat poisons are used in the garden and, if possible, that it is some distance from busy roads, criteria not easy to obtain in this day and age.

If you have to find a new release site, ensure it is already visited by hogs and that it can easily get out into other gardens. I do what is called soft release. This allows the hog the choice of either finding its own nest and food, or staying around for a while. The current nest should be contained in a cardboard box with a hole cut out. This should be placed under a shrub or in the undergrowth at the release site. The smell of its nest should reassure the animal for at least the first night.

An information leaflet for the recipient on what they should and should not do regarding the hog, would be very helpful, together with enough food, individually bagged for seven days, and a water dish.

In my experience very few hogs hang around. I can see in my mind's eye a hog's delight in being faced with all that freedom and their desire to distance themselves from those awful humans that kept them incarcerated. I have never experienced a tearful eye as a hog gives a long meaningful glance over its shoulder in grateful acknowledgement of what you have done for it. They either stay in the nest box or scuttle off, muttering under their breath, never to be seen again.

63. Can I keep releasing hogs into my garden?

Not a good idea as a garden can only sustain a certain number of hogs. To continually release at one site will simply mean others may be driven out in their quest for food. It is best to have a list of safe release sites; follow **No.62**. Obviously if you have a set of baby hogs that all came from one site, it is quite alright to release all of them back at that site.

64. How do I keep hogs in my garden safe from my dog at night?

Some dogs take great delight in hunting down hogs. To try and minimise this, either walk around the garden prior to letting your dog out or put on an outside light to 'scare' any hogs away that might be loitering around. Alternatively, simply keep the dog on a lead at night while you accompany it on its last call of nature. Mother hogs and babies tend to be the most vulnerable but they are usually only out in the garden from about August through to October, with possible autumn orphans in November.

65. It is early March and warm, should I wake it up?

I leave the hogs to wake when they feel ready, usually end of March. In the early days I did try to stimulate hogs to feed, but quickly found that if they are not ready they will not oblige. If the animal was small when it hibernated, weigh it, as the loss should only be ¼ of its original body weight. If more, then it should be placed on a heat pad and gently warmed up, offering it food and water when it is fully active. It will start huffing and breathing in deeply with a sound rather like bellows being drawn. It can take anything up to 2 hours to complete this process. The final stages are when it starts moving around and shivering in its attempt to speed up muscle warmth.

66. I think it is dying, the vet is closed, how can I put it out of its misery?

Keep trying to contact the vet. Legally a veterinary practice must provide 24-hour cover. They should be connected to an emergency number which may require you travelling some distance to find an open practice, but there is no other real alternative. To intentionally kill a hedgehog would contravene the Wildlife Act. It is also very difficult to dispatch a hog quickly and humanely.

In my first year, I had several hogs with what appeared to be severe injuries requiring euthanasia. If I had been able to put them to sleep I would have done so. However, being left with no other choice but to treat the animals, I was stunned to find that they responded to treatment, thrived and were eventually released back into the wild, thus showing that a second opinion is always worth seeking.

67. How do I dispose of dead bodies?

First make sure it is dead by waiting for rigor mortis to set in before sealing it in a polythene bag and taking it to the vet for incineration. Some vets may charge for this service, so don't be surprised if you are met with a small bill to pay. If you have access to clinical waste, ensure you have permission to use it for animal disposal.

68. How often should I clean the hutch?

This needs to be done once a day. Newspaper placed on the floor and, depending on its problems, either a towel or straw should be used for its nest site. Cover the nest with a plastic dome (available from pet shops) to give it the feeling of security. Leave the straw with the hog for anything up to a week, depending on how messy it is. The towel should be changed daily. Spray the hutch with *Milton* and wipe over before putting down fresh paper. Once a week scrub out and rinse the hutch before spraying it with *Milton*.

69. What is the best way to clean towels used for bedding?

You will have to ensure the towels have been thoroughly washed or there is a strong chance you will pass on diseases between animals. Firstly, use a large bucket to hand-wash them in a liquid wash, rinse them to get rid of all the solid matter and soak them for a couple of hours in a solution of *Milton*. You can then safely put them into your washing machine on a boil/heavy-soiled wash with no danger of passing anything on to man or beast.

70. Can I tame a hog and keep it as a pet?

Hogs dislike loud noises and sudden movements and they are naturally cautious of humans. You may get a wild hog to tolerate your presence while it feeds if you keep extremely still, but that is as far as it should go. If you were to hand-rear a hog that becomes happy being in your company you will unfortunately have to live with the fact that you have failed in caring for it properly, as the primary objective is always to release the animal back into the wild. Be aware of the health risks and the legalities regarding entrapment of wildlife; see **No.62**.

Autumn orphans and abandoned babies

A hog born in a given year must successfully reach 600 gm to hibernate. If it is in its second season or more then a higher hibernating weight may be required. Look at the hog; it should look rather like a balloon filled with water. If you hold it in your hands it should feel like an egg in an egg cup with its head small in proportion to its body. Also, if you gently jerk it up and down a couple of times in your hands its head and upper body should sink slightly into its main body.

The fat distribution is made up of white fat that is stored around the body to keep the hog 'ticking over' and red fat that is distributed almost like a jacket. It requires this super-charged red fuel to give it the boost to wake up from hibernation.

A late-born hog runs the risk of being abandoned by its mum who will leave the nest for a hibernation site, thus forcing her offspring to wander around frantically trying to look for food to gain weight. Autumn orphans can be found in distress at anything from about 150 gm in weight, feeding from the scattered remnants under bird tables.

I have found that nearly every hog brought in for care in this situation has an additional underlying health problem that requires treatment. I therefore do not advocate leaving the hog out in the wild to be fed from a feeding station. The hog should be kept in captivity either in a cage, hutch or enclosure, offered good quality food and then released at the end of April of the following year.

You may find it reaches 550 gm to 600 gm while in your care, thus reaching the ideal hibernating weight. This being the case, check its enclosure every day. If it is still feeding then clean it out and replenish its food. Be careful not to overfeed at this point. Keep its weight at below 800 gm as any more than this and you are in danger of creating an obese hog which will be vulnerable when released as it will be unable to fully curl up if attacked. There is also the additional burden of strain on the heart, lungs, kidneys, leg joints etc.

The first sign that a hog is getting ready to hibernate can be seen by a more thorough nest building activity, perhaps tearing up the paper from the bottom of its enclosure. It will dramatically reduce its consumption of food until it finally stops feeding. Always leave a bowl of water and a little dried food in the enclosure in case it wakes up hungry. Don't be tempted to keep checking the hog to see if it is ok—the more times you disturb it the more chance there is of you waking it up and causing it to use up its precious fat reserves.

Sometimes the hog has ideas of its own and the desire to hibernate is so strong that, despite its slight weight, it will still shut down and put itself into this torpid state. I have successfully hibernated hogs aged under 6 months at around 450 gm in a controlled environment. One went down at 390 gm dropping to 350 gm before waking up and feeding, finally reaching 690 gm before being released. Firstly, do not disturb an animal that has made this decision unless it is undergoing treatment. Ensure that it has access to dried food and water and check its enclosure every day for signs of activity. Usually it will hibernate for anything between a few days and a few weeks. It may wake up, eat some of the food and go back into hibernation again for a few days or a few weeks.

One old girl I had who was blind and only possessing her front teeth and a few stumps of her side teeth, decided to hibernate at 540 gm even though when she was admitted a few months earlier, I had succeeded in getting her up to a healthier 820 gm. She was extremely frail but I decided to respect her decision. I placed her in a hutch well padded out with straw and kept a check on her food bowl. She remained in this state for about 6 weeks before she finally surfaced and set about consuming a whole tin of food every night until she had reached 830 gm again. She then spent the rest of the winter intermittently hibernating and waking to consume vast amounts of food.

With experience, you will be able to recognise those that can be left to hibernate at the lower-than-recommended weight and those that must not be allowed to hibernate. If it is your first season with hogs I would strongly recommend trying your best to keep the animal awake if it is below the 600 gm for that year's offspring. Keeping the hog warm with a heat pad should be sufficient to fool the animal into thinking it is still time to stay awake.

Hogs will naturally wake every 6 to 11 days, though rarely leave their nests. They hibernate in a fully curled-up fashion, back upwards and head and tail towards the ground.

If the nest site becomes flooded or damaged, the hog will wake and move on to create another site. Obviously the more times it wakes and moves on, the more fat it will use up and the less likely it will be able to make it through winter.

An autumn orphan may come in with several problems. It will probably be hypothermic, dehydrated and emaciated, possibly suffering from myiasis, gut infection, lungworm infestation, ringworm and possibly intestinal worms. Do the usual checks from the beginning of **Problem solving, page 17.**

It is imperative that the hog has access to warmth during its first days or weeks in care. Electric heat pads are by far the best option as they provide a constant temperature. Ensure they have the space to move away from the heat if they want to. Remember, hot water bottles have a limited use as they require constant re-heating. A bottle that becomes cold will draw the heat away from the hog, so be vigilant in how you use this method.

All autumn orphan problems can be addressed with methods **No.1 to 93**. Simply look at the problems individually and follow each stage through. It is very easy when faced with a 'conveyor belt' of young hogs all exhibiting the same problems to forget to look deeper for other causes.

Nests abandoned earlier in the year present different problems, mostly babies which are a much smaller size and less developed. You might have to toilet the hoglets, clean them and bottle-feed them regularly day and night. Warmth, again, is essential. Rehydrating the hog is the first priority. Once this has been achieved introduce *Esbilac/Cimivit*, depending on the age of the hog; see **pages 57** and **58**.

How old is the hog?

Use the following guide to determine a hog's age.

Birth:	blind, deaf, bald, 7 gm to 25 gm
1 hour:	white prickles emerge through the protective blister covering its skin (see photo on **page 72**)
36 hours:	second coat of prickles emerging, dark brown and white, thinner than the adult's spines
5 days:	dark spines outnumber the white ones
11 days:	may start to practise curling up
2 weeks:	eyes opening, third set of prickles emerging
3 weeks:	eyes and ears now fully open, first upper incisors erupting
4 weeks:	snout pointed, milk teeth showing, now weighing between 85 gm to 130 gm
6 to 8 weeks:	normally accompanies mum on foraging trips
8 weeks:	should weigh about 350 gm, could leave mum at any time now
3 to 4 months:	milk teeth replaced by permanent teeth
5 months:	sexually mature although will not mate until the following year
3 to 5 years:	life-span in the wild (a captive hog can live up to 8 years)

Feeding plan for babies

One method for determining the daily volume of milk required by a hog is to weigh the hog and divide its weight by 4, which gives the daily amount of milk required in millilitres (ml). For example, a hog that weighs 30 gm will require about 8 ml of milk over 24 hours. Now decide how old the hog is and calculate how much milk it should have for each feed based on the number of feeds required per day. Another method is to follow **No.75**. Read **No.78** before attempting any feeding.

Under 8 days:	feed every 2 hours day and night using the above method
8 to 14 days:	every 3 hours from 7 am to 11 pm
2 to 3 weeks:	every 3 to 4 hours from 7 am to 11 pm
3 to 4 weeks:	as above and offer a shallow dish of *Esbilac/Cimivit* to lap
4 to 5 weeks:	reduce hand-feeds and offer liquidised solids together with the milk and water
5 to 6 weeks:	phase out hand-feeds and milk, offer food mashed instead of liquidised
6 weeks:	should now be on solids with no human contact other than cleaning out its environment
8 weeks:	should now weigh 350 gm to 450 gm.

I have not managed to rear babies that come in weighing under 30 gm. There appears to be a cut-off point where viability is too low, possibly due to the absence of mum's colostrum.

I have also noticed that hoglets under 40 gm fail to survive if any one of their toes turns completely black. I am not sure if this is coincidence or a symptom of impending mortality.

71. Babies wandering about during the day

Babies that have left the nest in search of mum are usually in distress. Gather them up and wrap them in a small tea towel. They will require constant external heat for the first 4 to 5 weeks of age. Check for fly eggs and maggots in the same way you would an adult (**No.11**, **No.12**, **No.13** and **No.14**). You might find that the eyes and ears are still closed if they are only a week or so old.

72. Found one baby, could there be more?

Hogs tend to give birth to 3 to 5 babies on average although they have been known to have litters of up to 7. One baby hog on its own is extremely rare, so keep looking and listening for possible siblings. With experience you may be able to guess roughly how large the litter is simply by comparing how developed the baby's head is to the size of its body. A large, well-developed head on a small body indicates a large nest of babies, whereas a large head on a large body indicates fewer babies.

73. A nest of babies is abandoned under a shed, how do I get them out?

Even the smallest of babies is capable of crawling around. If it is impossible to gain access to the nest and if you are sure they have been abandoned, you could try leaving either a saucer of *goat's milk, milk for kittens*, or *tinned cat or dog food,* depending on the age of the babies. Once they smell this, hopefully they will make their way towards the food or milk. Proceed with **No.75** and **No.78**.

74. What food should babies eat?

Refer to **No.78** before you give any milk and **pages 57** and **58** to ascertain the age and development of the hog. If the hog is still on a liquid diet the best milk to use is *Esbilac* which unfortunately is extremely difficult and expensive to obtain, although Spike's World stock it. A cheaper alternative is *Cimivit* which is available from most vets and should be prepared as directed on the tin. Into either the *Esbilac* or *Cimivit*, add *Abidec vitamins*, available from your pharmacy in the baby section. One drop per day per hog is sufficient. Feeding should be through a pipette or special small-mammal feeding bottle. You should be able to get the bottle from your vet or Spike's World and the pipette from any craft shop (they are usually used to transfer glass paint to a dish). Whichever feeding method you use, ensure you wash and sterilise the equipment thoroughly after each feed.

75. What is the routine for feeding?

Refer to **No.78** before proceeding with a feed.

Rule of thumb is to give the baby hog a ¼ of its body weight in milk over 24 hours, feeding from 7 am to about 11 pm with about 2 to 5 hours gap between feeds, depending on its age and condition. Check **'How old is the hog?' page 57** against **'Feeding plan for babies', page 58**.

Alternatively, the method I use which offers a very good rate of success is to weigh the hog prior to feeding and weigh it again after the feed. There should be a gain of about 2 gm. Check its weight before each feed. Follow this method only when the hog is about 11 days old. A younger hog should be fed using the first method, to avoid bloating.

Make up a feed that will, hopefully, last the whole day. This can be stored in the fridge for a maximum of 24 hours; throw away any old milk. Weigh the hog and make a note on its records. This needs to be noted once a day before you start feeding in the morning. It should have gained anything from 1 gm to 3 gm since the weight taken 24 hours previously. Don't panic if it has lost weight while you are on the second or third day, as it can take a while for the hog to get used to feeding from a bottle at fixed feeding times, rather than on demand from its mother. Try reducing the time between feeds if there is a weight loss. Bear in mind a baby hog has a tiny stomach that holds very little.

Hold the hog upright or on its back in the palm of your hand, whichever is easiest and then offer it milk at body temperature. Be patient and gentle, it soon gets the hang of it. Either insert the pipette/feeding teat into the side of the mouth and move it to the front in traditional feeding fashion or place directly in the front of the mouth. Some like to have the milk drizzled into their mouth and they simply lap it down, others guzzle it down in great gulping motions. When you have finished, weigh the hog again. Depending on its age it should have gained anything up to 3 gm.

Toileting the hog is essential for the first three weeks of its life. The mother will stimulate bladder movement by licking the baby's tail area. You will have to emulate this by using the corner of a wet tissue and quickly but lightly flick this area till the hoglet empties its bladder and possibly its bowels. Do this at the end of every feed. Then use a baby-wipe suitable for sensitive skin (half of one is more than sufficient), to wipe the face, neck, body and finally the tail area.

Hogs in care are prone to sore tails, hind feet and toes, due to urine scald. Particular care should be taken to massage oil into this area. I find the best is *Aloe Vera gel* + *vitamin E,* a clear jelly used for human babies' skin. Then pop the hoglet away till its next feed when you will weigh it again before repeating the feeding method described above.

76.I have fed the baby and its abdomen has started to expand dramatically

This could be bloat and unfortunately the situation is usually irreversible. *Fennel tea*, if used in the early stages of feeding, should help prevent this; see **No. 78**. There is little that can be done to alleviate this problem other than withholding milk feeds for 24 hours and then repeating the rehydration regime in **No.78**. However, death is the usual outcome.

77. Tail/anus/toes are bright red/bleeding

Urine scald is very painful for the baby hog. Ensure you wipe the hog efficiently. Massage *Aloe Vera gel* + *vitamin E* into its skin, toes and tail when you first receive the hog to prevent this problem arising. Reduce toileting to every other feed and try to toilet the hog so the urine runs away from the sore areas. You should be able to quickly get this under control. *Sudocreme* can be used, but I find it does not stick to the hog's skin once it has become sore. Prevention is always better than cure so ensure the hog is well oiled from day one.

78. Skin looks very wrinkled on tummy

A sure sign of dehydration and indicates it has been on its own for some time. Proceed with caution. Because it has not fed for a while, the trick here is to rehydrate before giving food or milk. First decide how old it is by following the guide on **page 57**. Make up blackcurrant *Dioralyte* as per directions on the packet with *fennel tea* instead of plain water (1 teabag to 1 pint of warm water). Add 1 drop of *Abidec* per hog. The following rehydration regime should help to prevent bloat and put the hog in a fit state to accept milk or solids.

First 4 hours of care:	fennel-mix every ½ hour according to size of hog; toilet at the beginning of the first feed, 2 hours later and again at the end (notice the change in the colour of the urine from dark orange to a clear liquid).
4 to 8 hours of care:	fennel-mix every hour; toilet every 2 hours.
8 to 24 hours of care:	fennel-mix and toilet every 3 hours.

The hog should now be ready to accept *Esbilac/Cimivit*. Again, little and often is best, slowly increasing according to their needs. After the initial 14 hours you should be able to follow the feeding plan according to the hog's age and development; see **pages 57** and **58**.

79. How often do I feed the baby?

Refer to the feeding plan on **page 58**.

80. At what age should I stop toileting the baby?

Keep toileting for the first 2 to 3 weeks of age or until their eyes open. Note that baby female hogs may take longer than males to reach this point.

81. Droppings look like little green eggs

Quite normal. When a baby hog is on a milk diet its stools will look like this. They change as its diet changes from milk to meat.

82. Baby has been feeding well, but next morning it is floppy and flat

It may not be warm enough; ensure it has access to a heat pad. Or, you may have a runt which, even if it is with its mother, will not survive.

83. Can I put two litters of babies together and use the same feeding bottle?

Never mix litters. The babies' immune systems will be low already from not getting milk from their mother. The last thing you want is a gut infection to spread through them all. Similarly, if you share a feeding bottle between two nests, you are very likely to pass on possible infections.

I use a different bottle for each litter, washing and sterilising after all the babies in that nest have finished their feed, thus ensuring it is always germ free.

84. When do I take the heat pad away?

Try removing the heat pad when they are about 4 weeks old. Check every hour to start with to ensure that they are able to maintain their own body temperature. If not, replace the heat source and try again after a few days.

85. How do I wean from milk to meat?

When a baby's eyes first open, offer a shallow dish (a Pringles lid is ideal) with *Esbilac/Cimivit* for it to lap from. Carry on feeding by hand as its first experiences of milk in a dish tend to be of a Cleopatra style; they often bathe in it rather than feed!

Once it has mastered lapping, at about 21 days of age, liquidise some *chicken cat food* with *Esbilac/Cimivit*. Pour a little into the dish, offering water in a separate dish. Make enough food for the day and keep the extra refrigerated, remembering to warm it up before offering to the hog.

Check its droppings. If they become very liquid, stop feeding meat and go back to milk, then leave for a couple of days before re-introducing meat to its diet.

Another way to tell if the hogs are ready for solids is when an otherwise steady gain in weight is replaced with a loss. This is a good indication that they are ready for food with substance. Continue with the *Abidec* at 1 drop per baby per day. If you place a couple of lumps of meat in the food bowl each day they will start by simply playing with it before eventually tucking in. They are now ready to accept food that is mashed up.

86. Baby's eyes are starting to open but have a discharge

Not uncommon. With cotton wool soaked in *Optrex* simply wipe from the outside corner to the inside edge of the eye. After a couple of wipes the eye should be clean and open. Keep a check on this over the next few days.

87.How do I distance myself from the hog so it can be successfully released back into the wild?

Follow a simple but effective routine. You will have to accept that in the early days while bottle-feeding and toileting, you are going to handle this hog on a regular basis. It will probably start calling to you when it hears your voice and it will get very excited when you put your hand into its enclosure. Don't concern yourself about inadvertently taming it at this stage. As long as handling is done simply to feed and toilet, you will not be making an unbreakable bond with the baby.

I usually put a hog into a hutch once it no longer requires heat and bottle-feeding and is on solids, so you will naturally not be in contact as often. It will, however, still call for you when you approach the hutch. Be firm with it, let it sniff your fingers and chew your hand but refrain from picking it up.

The final port of call before releasing the hog is to place it into a pen. This should have woodchip on the ground and a nest site consisting of perhaps a rabbit nesting dome. Straw should be placed into this, and the hog encouraged to add to the nest by providing it with extra bedding. A hog will dig into the woodchip looking for mini beasts to feed on, which will help develop its ability to forage successfully when released back into the wild. Continue to feed at nights but reduce the daytime feed to only a couple of pieces of dried food per hog. The contact you have will quickly diminish and you should have a hog that runs and hides when you approach its run. You can then congratulate yourself on a job very well done and having a hog that is ready to go back to the wild where it belongs.

88.When can I release it?

In the wild a hog will be about 350 gm before it wanders off from its mother. In captivity I wait until they are 450 gm in the summer as this gives them every possible chance of survival; follow **No.62**. If it is an autumn release, being any time up to mid-November, 600 gm is the optimum weight.

89.Hog I have been caring for appears stiff and hardly moves

This should only occur in the winter months when the hog has decided to hibernate. As long as the hog has been active and is a good weight then you should allow it to continue its hibernation. Carefully remove any soiled paper and bedding from its enclosure, replace with clean fresh food and water, then simply keep an eye on it. It may wake up a few times before finally committing itself to hibernation. Do not be tempted to keep disturbing it, as each time it reacts to your presence it will be using up valuable fat reserves.

90.Over-wintered hog has very long claws, is that normal?

If the hog has not hibernated and has been kept in a cage or hutch it will, in all probability, have grown very long claws. These are usually kept at a manageable level in the wild by digging for food. Trim the ends as directed in **No.23** prior to releasing.

91.Can I put several unrelated hogs together?

This is not recommended for several reasons. They could pass on undetected diseases; they may fight; they might mate. Hogs from the same nest will mate if left together until the spring and so should be separated in January. If they are together in the winter months the active hogs might continually disturb a hog as it tries to hibernate, thus causing it to lose weight dramatically.

92.Can I release all hogs at the same time?

Not ideal, as one of the hogs may decide that the nest and food bowl belongs to itself. You will then have a situation where additional hogs will have to leave to make their own nest and forage for food. This defeats the objective of soft release; see **No.62**.

93.When does the breeding season start?

It is a good idea to know roughly what is happening during the year with wild hogs so that you have some idea as to what you are likely to be faced with:

April:	hogs wake up and start to put on weight.
May (end of):	mating commences; 5 week gestation period.
June/July:	babies are born and stay with mum for about 8 weeks.
August/September:	babies should now be independent and putting on weight ready for hibernation.
November:	hibernation commences.

You can see from the above that timing is critical. If a mother loses or abandons her first litter, for whatever reason, and has a second litter, she is in real danger of running out of time and will hibernate before she has successfully reared her young. We are then left with autumn orphans wandering around trying to find sufficient food to grow and lay down fat at a time when their natural food supply is diminishing.

Hog story

Harriet, a very old hedgehog

Looking at her spines you can see that they are predominantly ginger instead of black, grey and cream. Her skin colour has started to change to pink around her throat and upper arms. Her side teeth are worn to stumps.

Harriett was admitted underweight and had lost her sight in both eyes. It was obvious that the loss of one eye was an old injury she had learned to live with; the other was more recent. The complete loss of her sight caused her to come out during the day and, as far as she was concerned no one could see her. She went about her business in blissful ignorance of her visibility.

Harriett was very willing to be fed by hand and would home in on any carer who entered her enclosure. Failure to produce food would result in her biting your fingers and trying to drag you away. We soon learned who was the boss and to show her some respect.

Hogs are naturally solitary animals, only coming together to mate. Harriett's behaviour was very unusual for a wild hog but typical of hogs kept in captivity. When an old male hog was introduced to her enclosure suffering from a neurological disorder and unable to multi-task, love hearts flew in all directions from our cantankerous old girl. It became an obvious problem for poor old Conundrum as she continually circled him, causing him to fall over in confusion and remain prostrate till she finally settled down and lay by his side. After a few weeks she realised he was not 'up to the job' and so changed her tactics. Every time he fell over she would dash off to one of the nest sites, dragging straw out in her mouth, and commence nest building wherever he lay. It became quite a game for Conundrum, trying to find tiny, out-of-the-way corners where Harriett could not venture.

There were five nest boxes available in this enclosure where the geriatrics are placed to live out their final days. It is interesting to observe that in this type of situation hogs accept each other quite willingly, to the extent that they all try to squeeze into the same nest box. It could be that the ready supply of food and the abundance of available nest sites remove the characteristics of a solitary hog's life. Certainly, if you provide enough food for cats you will increase the number that can comfortably live in one house, so it is not too unreasonable to apply this train of thought to hedgehogs.

Albino hogs are very rare

Their lack of skin pigmentation produces a hog with pink skin and red eyes, unlike blond hogs which have black eyes.

The immune system of albinos is lower than a normal hog and this, together with it being easily predated upon, dramatically reduces its chances of survival in the wild. I follow the same release plan as with a non-releasable hog and find a safe, enclosed garden for it to live out its life; see **No.61**.

Hog cases

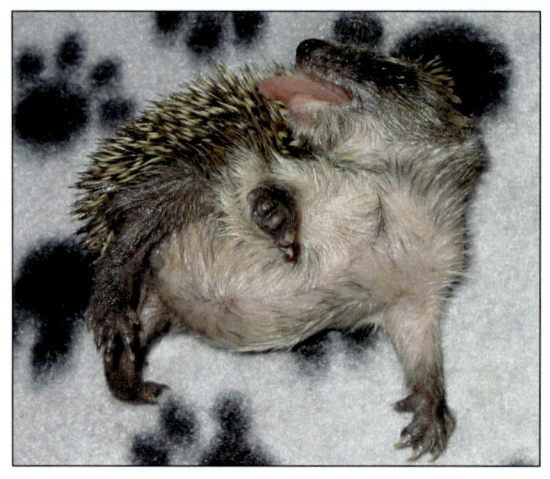

A young hog, having tasted the leather strap on a carer's watch, starts *self-anointing*. This can be a little unsettling to witness but it is quite normal behaviour. It is not known why hogs perform this strange ritual but every hog I have hand-reared has exhibited this trait.

Below is a hog with typical ringworm symptoms. The fur on its underbelly, skirt, arms and legs has fallen out leaving only a Mohican hairstyle on the

top of its head. The skin around the skirt often becomes cracked and bleeds. Rubbing *Tea-tree ointment* around the skirt helps soften the skin and enables the hog to move more comfortably. Use in conjunction with *Imaverol* to quickly get this condition under control.

In this picture you can easily see the muscle that runs around the skirt. This works like a draw-string bag, holding the hog tightly in its protective spine-covered skin.

This hog has an obvious broken leg which has reset itself, albeit at a disturbing angle. He was underweight and suffering from sarcoptic mange on the side of the damaged limb. Any hog that is unable to groom itself sufficiently is in danger of building up a heavy burden of parasites. As this hog was not damaging his foot by using it, I decided to release him into an enclosed garden where his carer was able to groom him with a scrubbing brush in a flicking motion from the nape of his neck to his back leg, a sensation hogs tend to enjoy once they learn to trust you.

Quite often I receive a hog which is covered in ticks. Ticks should be removed as quickly as possible. The use of a tick gadget is by far the easiest, quickest and most efficient method. If there are too many for you to comfortably deal with without stressing the animal, concentrate on the easiest to remove first. You could simply remove the lighter-coloured ticks first as they are still filling with blood; the black ones are already engorged and should soon fall off.

Ticks are related to spiders and have the same climbing abilities, so ensure you wipe the sides of the cage to remove any escapees when you clean the nest out.

Baby hogs

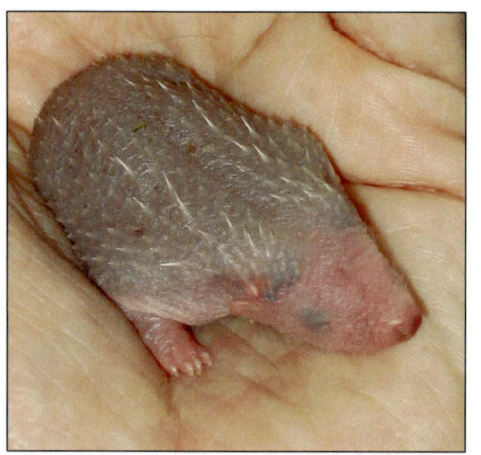

This tiny hog was born in captivity and was attacked by its mum. The first picture shows it at only a few hours old. The second picture was taken two hours later. By the end of the day it had a full covering of small white spines over its back.

Even at such a tiny size, baby hogs will leave their nest in search of mum. This hog still had his eyes and ears closed and had not cut his baby teeth when he was found staggering around during the day. The noise babies make when in distress is unmistakable, sounding rather like a cross between a sparrow and a budgie with attitude! Always check for more babies as mum usually gives birth to between 3 and 5 offspring.

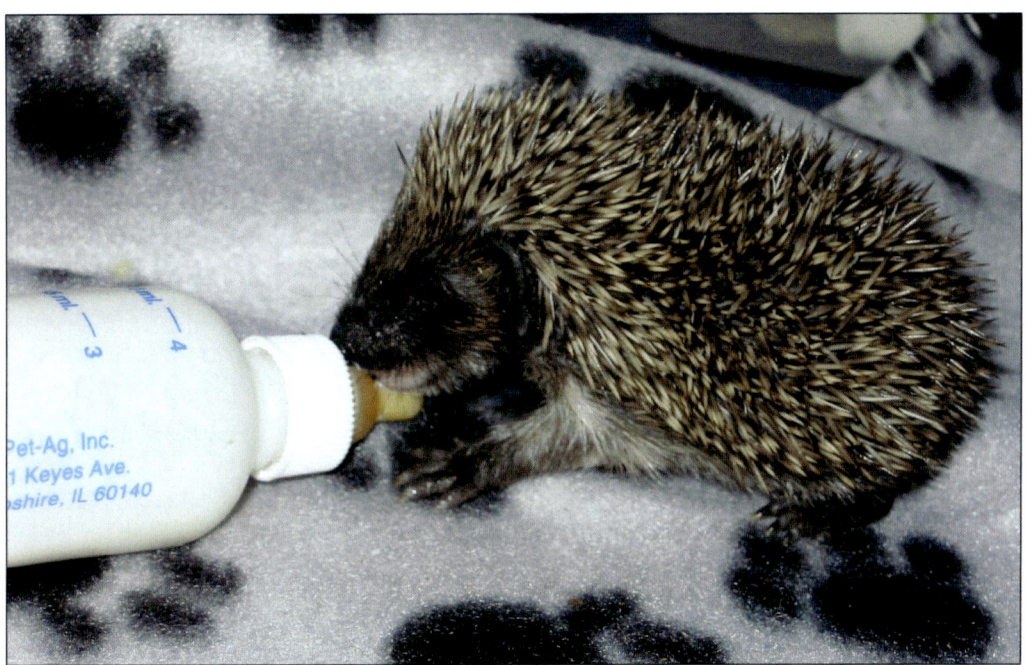

Feeding babies is easiest using a feeding bottle, although pipettes and syringes are very effective. Use formula milk for puppies or kittens (*Esbilac/Cimivit*), obtainable from vets, pet shops or Spike's World. Alternatively, goat's milk can be utilised in an emergency or if you have only one baby that requires milk for a couple of days.

All feeding equipment should be sterilised, before and after use. Milk should be served at body temperature. Discard any milk remaining after each feed. Throw away any milk that has been stored in the fridge for over 24 hours. A jug of hot water to stand the bottle in is the easiest method of ensuring the milk is served at the correct temperature. Each time you use the bottle, check that it has not become too hot or cold, by dripping a little of the formula onto your wrist.

Summary

Hogs, like all creatures, are individuals, responding in different ways to different treatments. Some of the suggested remedies and courses of action might be met with a hog that does not respond immediately. Patience is quite often the answer, together with time, a commodity we unfortunately don't have the luxury of in many cases.

Bear in mind, once you have successfully treated one set of symptoms it is not uncommon to be met with a further list to solve. This is because when an animal becomes ill its immune system is usually weak, leaving it wide open to infection from anything else that might be going around, or allowing a manageable condition the hog is harbouring to take hold and become a problem. It is also very important for you to find a sympathetic vet, as without their guidance and drugs it will be an impossible task to successfully care for a hog long-term.

No hog, unless it has serious mobility problems (in which case you should be questioning its quality of life and why you are keeping it alive), should be housed in a hutch or rabbit pen for the duration of its life as they require much more space to move around, exercise and explore. In the wild they can easily cover between 2 to 3 miles in an evening.

Regarding hogs in enclosed gardens: the final outcome for these animals will, in all probabilities, be a sad one. If your domestic pet were to become ill you would usually notice this within 24 hours. A hog in an enclosed garden is still a wild animal and, as such, will not be fussed over in the same way your pets are. Possibly the first sign of a hog's difficulties might be finding it collapsed on your lawn, days if not weeks after the initial problem started. Please bear in mind if you are faced with this type of scenario that 1) this is the natural end to all hedgehogs living in the wild and 2) the hog would in all probability have died long ago without the security of your garden. There is only so much you can do to safeguard the welfare of your nocturnal guest.

You might be faced with a possible run of failures. Don't become disillusioned. Keeping a list of all hogs brought in gives you the opportunity to look back at your successes. Before-and-after photographs are always a good boost to morale when you are feeling low.

The old hogs kept in captivity at Caddington Hedgehogs form a special bond with the carers and when a hog inevitably dies it can be a very upsetting time. You will have to learn to harden yourself to these situations as they are obviously going to occur with the type of cases involved. The day you stop caring *about* your hedgehogs is the day you should stop caring *for* them.

Record any phone numbers of useful contacts, such as vets, other carers etc, below.

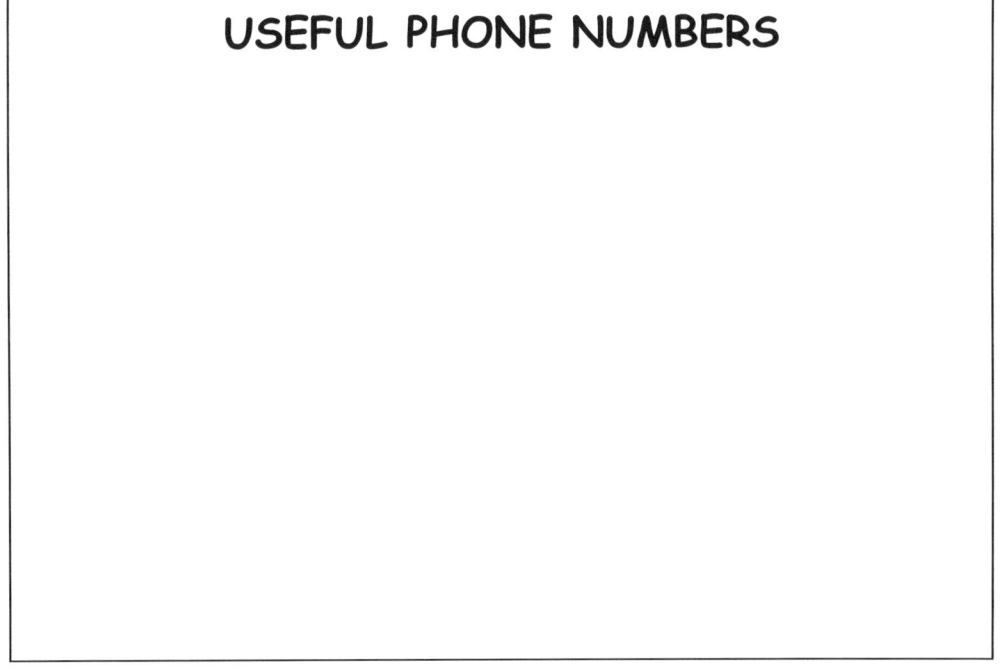

The Message Pad on the following page can be photo-copied for your use.

MESSAGE PAD

Name   Phone number

Location

Problem

Action

Bibliography

It is important to further your knowledge of hedgehogs by reading as much as you possibly can on their care and secret life. Listed below are some books that are essential reading if you intend to start caring for hedgehogs.

Hedgehog Rehabilitation
by Kay Bullen VN

British Hedgehog
Preservation Society

Hedgehogs
by Nigel Reeve

T & A.D. Poyser

The Natural Hedgehog
by Lenni Sykes

Gaia Books Ltd

The Complete Hedgehog
by Les Stocker

Chatto & Windus/London

Hedgehogs
by Pat Morris

Whittet Books